Only Knew

BY JOANIE LAURER

WITH MICHAEL ANGELI

CollinsWillow

An Imprint of HarperCollins*Publishers*

First published in the United States in 2001
by HarperCollins*Publishers*
10 East 53rd St
New York NY 10022

This edition published in 2001
by Collins Willow
an imprint of HarperCollins*Publishers*
London

1 3 5 7 9 8 6 4 2

The Collins Willow website address is:
www.**fire**and**water**.com/sport

A CIP catalogue record for this book is available from the British Library

ISBN 0 00 710669 6

Printed and bound in Great Britain by The Bath Press

Contents

CHYNA

Introduction

Joanie Loves Chyna

I am smiling. I can see my reflection in the glass security door—to look at me, you'd think I was sucking on a pacifier dipped in Honey instead of a Power Bar that tastes like chalk. Clouds, rain, and chills in Vancouver, where the sun is just a bit player—are you kidding me, it's freakin' June out there! Twenty thousand mat maniacs are here for the taping of *Raw Is War,* waiting to show their tonsils, proposition me, paw at my hair, toss their house keys in the ring—I got hit in the front tooth once—and I am smiling. I have a blister on my foot that could irrigate half of Death Valley, a room in a hotel crawling with tipped-off fans, a rental car without GPS, and that's just fine, because I am lost in a great big won-the-lottery, I-got-rhythm Buick of a smile. Ten minutes before I go on and the costume lady needs to repair Too Cool's jeans before she can take in the butt on my leather hot pants—they got stretched out when Kurt Angle tried to ring-toss me in Peoria—but I am smiling, smiling with a thousand and one reasons not to.

Come on, take a little stroll through the ass end of the arena with me and I'll show you what I mean. This is where I exist: in dank, cavernous, giant-size garages and hangars. Cement—the official color of the WWF. Communication trailers, a jungle river of cables, racks of sweat-stained, fraying costumes, the acrid stench of Ho' perfume mingled

CHYNA

with Sports Cream, and exhaust fumes from The Undertaker's Hog. Hungry? There's a soiled picnic table with some fingered-over generic party mix, stale tortilla chips, precut carrot sticks, and a few sticks of gum—you want atmosphere? Go to Denny's. Those wrestlers over there, looking more gray than the folding chairs they're slumped on? They just found out they'll be idle tonight, the writers didn't include them in the lineup. An hour earlier, they were like the rest of us—tense, wondering, hoping. Lots of apprehension, kind of like waiting to see if you're going to the front in a war. Only you *want* to go to the front. If you're not picked, everyone knows it, everyone shies away from it, and suddenly the wrestling world is a cancer ward, a hostel where the truth is handled with care. Tonight those poor beat-up bastards are dead before the battle. And me? To them, I'm just another body taking up space on the lifeboat. Same thing, different city, five-plus nights a week—somebody draws the short straw, someone gets left out, somebody gets the shaft, and I feel for them. They're not family, but damn close, and on any other night, the sight of them waddling back to the locker room in sandals, their very muscles wilted, gets me down—me, a person with abandonment issues that a crate of Paxil and ten years' worth of psychotherapy couldn't put a dent in. The last time I saw my mother I was sixteen, and she was draped

CHINA *Introduction*

over the hood of my car. My father, who never got over my decision not to join the FBI, is getting even by selling bits and pieces of me over the Internet. At last he's making money this time. And there's my live-in boyfriend, Paul Levesque, a.k.a. Triple H, a.k.a. Hunter. I mentioned the word "commitment" a few weeks ago, and now he's walking around looking terrified, like someone's following him. Big deal. Tonight even he'll be upstaged, because Kid Rock is performing just before The Undertaker's bout. Wrestling and hip-hop—a match made in hell. That's okay, too. Smile on, little girl, smile on.

That lanky babe over there, talking to our talent coordinator? Six feet tall, cowboy hat, got the *Total Request Live* attitude working, the Internet fantasy body, nineteen-inch Lara Croft waist, 36D funbags, and sipping a can of diet Mountain Dew (probably her dinner)? She wants to replace me. Oh, sure, she'll end up handing out cosmetics at Bloomingdale's or serving drinks in a cone hat at Medieval Times, but the next Chyna, the next Ninth Wonder of the World? C'mon. They show up in every city. "I'm here to wrestle, hopefully," I overheard her say to someone. Yeah, right. "Fire in the hole!" The Rock yells, and the pyro explosions they use to announce Kane entering the arena cause Miss Fat-Tits to spill her Mountain Dew on her imitation-alligator cowboy boots. Yeah, I'm smiling. I'm smiling even though I

CHYNA

just read in *Talk* magazine that I am now six-feet-two instead of five-ten, I am smiling even though I'm on the front page of the *Globe,* with the caption WRESTLER'S BOOB EXPLODES, I'm smiling (just barely, believe me) even though some lady just cornered me in the bathroom, slapped a pen in my palm, and demanded an autograph. I'm on—gotta go, lady.

"MAMACITA!" the taped voice calls out—that's my current introduction—"Ma-ma-cita!" The voice is all greased and baby-talky, as if uttered by a bandito with a gold tooth. The audience hears it and they break into a crazy cheer; I hear it and usually I swear to myself that after the match I'm gonna find the guy who owns that voice and tear his vocal cords out. The Rock gets "CAN YOU SMELL WHAT THE ROCK IS COOKING?" Hunter gets "Rage Against the Machine." I get "Mamacita," but tonight I hear "Mamacita" and it's music to my ears. My stage partner, the Mexican wrestler Eddie "Latino Heat" Guerrero, hands me a dozen roses. Doesn't matter that they smell like old celery. Doesn't matter that he gets to wrestle Kurt Angle and I'm pretty much there for moral support. Oh, yeah, I get to blindside Angle in the crotch when he's not looking, maybe rake my fingernails across his face from behind, but mainly I'm the boy-toy, and, in fact, have been for a few weeks now. Doesn't matter that I have enough going on to snap both their nuts off and give them

CHINA *Introduction*

a hard-on at the same time. You know what? I couldn't be happier. You could use my head to floss Rakishi's butt and tonight nothing could bring me down.

Okay, I'm *supposed* to smile—you could argue that and you'd be pretty much right. My character, Chyna? She used to be a villain, a bad guy, a heel. Lately, the mandate coming from above—that would be the McMahon family—is that I will be a good guy, a babyface, which actually has its rewards. When I was a heel? Fans chucked batteries at me instead of house keys. They spit, throw pennies at you, spill beer on your outfit. You know what? Even that would be fine—I'd still be smiling. In the immortal words of Popeye, I am what I am—a woman of substance, a lady with muscle, and I, Joanie Laurer, can't even stop Chyna. You see, some people are meant to be doctors, some people are meant to be mothers, or split the atom, sing, dance, walk on the moon, make money, herd cattle, catch footballs, write lines of computer code, speak lines of dialogue, fly, crawl, sail, or just plain sit and watch. Me? I was meant to be somebody else. And don't let anybody kid you—having two faces for the world to see is a good thing. Getting there? Well, that's a longer story . . .

CHYNA *Introduction*

1

Everything Is Preordained

Most people start from the beginning:

Miss A was born in the city of B, raised by hardworking, middle-class parents who only wanted the best for Miss A, spent wonderful Indian summers with loving grandparents, graduated with honors, saw the world, settled down, married C, had little D's and E's. Most people embrace a history of themselves for the very reason that it is embraceable—in wrestling it's called playing to somebody's strength. Certainly, I have a past—that I'll get to in due time—and some of it is even embraceable. Hey, I went to a prestigious high school, didn't I? My grandparents had a boat, right? And fathers? I had three, possibly four, if you count the boyfriend in between who never married my mom. What I have then, more than fond memories, are acknowledgments. Look, I was always a big, different . . . *visible* girl. Heads turned in the third-grade cafeteria (I lived with it), heads turned at the Emmys (I gave them the finger). My life is roughly (ha ha) divided into three parts: Being different and hating it. Being different and accepting it. Being different and, well, embracing it. And the embracing began with a kiss.

Independence Day 1995 God, I look great in a uniform! Standing in front of the closet-door mirror, I am a beaming approximation of a prim and professional

CHYNA

flight attendant—tight skirt cut at mid-thigh, wrinkle-free blue blazer, white blouse, looking a little underinflated, frankly (the miracle of the saline baggie would come later), but I make up for it in legs, tensed by two-inch pumps. And, be honest, now—can anybody other than a teamster resist my seductive Prince Valiant 'do? "Knock them dead, Joanie Laurer, knock them dead!" my neighbor, Maxine, shouts as I'm climbing into my car. "Hope you get the belt!" she called out, doing the pantomime of some freaky house-wife superhero, her hands raised over her head, joining them together as if she were plugging in all the juice needed to light the Florida Keys into an extension cord. Yeah, the belt. Back in flight school everyone wanted to do the belt thing, that little preflight demonstration where you show everybody on the plane how the seat belts buckle. I had just completed a six-week class, training to become a flight attendant—a class of about thirty bubbly hopefuls of both sexes. Most of them were my age, early to mid-twenties, with a couple of divorcées sprinkled in, hiding their forties behind face putty and Jackie O glasses—I actually liked the older ones the most because they knew shame. The ones my age had that typical sense of entitlement, that slacker, world-weary thing going on, as if saying, "Gimme the damn job already, so I can get on with the hating of everything about it." When graduation time comes (if you're con-

Everything Is Preordained

scious, you graduate), everyone's forgotten everything about safety, inflatable life jackets, where to blow, the psychology of handling some drunken rock star who wants to crap in the coffee service cart—but not the belt, not the demonstration. Even the most jaded, bullshit-slinging, bored, Tetris-playing, tanning losers sat up when the belt was mentioned. And that first time when you're chosen? Wow. You're the point man. Everyone on the freaking plane immediately knows there's something extra-special about you. They may not pay attention, but believe me, they know you're not just some run-of-the-mill pillow fluffer, right? Of course, I'd be lucky if the planes even had seat belts. My new job was with some outfit now out of business whose name we will withhold anyway. I mean, these guys were way below ValuJet, we're talking bottom of the barrel here. And I couldn't have cared less. Because I've had a lot of jobs. I was a cocktail waitress in a stripper bar and still have bruises on my ass from the pinches of slumming Cuban nationals. I sang in a bar band (when the drummer showed up) and never made a penny. This was before I got clotheslined in the throat so many times that I lost my voice. I fell asleep manning a 900-number chat line, where one guy paid $2.99 a minute to have me listen to him blow his nose into his ex-wife's underpants. (And what a nose. He stayed on the line for a half-hour.) I had more bad jobs

CHYNA

than Manpower. But this? Finally I was going in the right direction—in a brand-new ride, I might add. Yeah, I bought a new car, trading in the Jeep Cherokee that said, "Mountain climber, into campfires, hiking, looking for enduring relationship w/clean, hetero male," for a Ford Probe that spoke of futons, sushi, self-actualization, the piercing-the-tiger position, and take me to your leader! The sky was the limit! Exciting places to go to, people to meet—maybe a marriage proposal from some high-powered commodities broker? Okay, so I was probably selling myself a little short. I knew the job wasn't nearly as glamorous as I wanted it to be, but I could do worse. Hey— a steady paycheck. Benefits. Money. The *belt* . . .

If you live in the Florida Keys, there's literally only one way to get to Miami and beyond. Route 1, which eventually becomes Interstate 1, runs on the spine of the Florida Keys, then swings northwest, up a stretch of causeway not much wider than The Rock's cocked eyebrow. I'd driven the stretch hundreds of times, and the worst part of it—for me—was driving at night in frog-spawning season. Thousands of them, crossing the causeway. They *pop* when you run over them. So it's two lanes, running north and south, at one point narrowing to two hundred yards between Blackwater Sound to the west and Barnes Sound to the east. Other places it gets wide enough to accommo-

CHYNA

date a gas station or a hamburger joint. And that's where the trouble starts. Water on both sides of you, fog, desolation, it's easy to get disoriented. We call them ghost riders—people who pull off for something, get all turned around, and pull back onto the wrong side of the causeway.

I remember thinking about cellos just before it happened—how I used to love to play the cello, my instrument of choice in school, and how big and unwieldy it was. But there was something feminine about it, too—the curves, the shape, the way you held it, etc. And I had this Patty Loveless cassette playing on the car stereo. Country-western music, which I absolutely hated, but the guitar player in my band wanted to cover some of her songs, and I, with my pack-rat, never-burn-bridges mentality, figured I could keep up my brilliant singing career between flights to Paris, Cairo, and Rome. Cellos and country-western music. Reaching for a Diet Coke from my nifty new Probe cup holders, I remember thinking, "Joanie, you are a chick with a lot of shit that doesn't fit together," when I saw the car, expanding in my windshield. And he was so close, coming on so fast, that when I slammed on the brakes it sounded like *that* made the sound of the crash—metal crunching, engines thrown out of kilter, motor mounts tearing away, plastic ripping, all of it alive, violent, and jagged. In this weird compression of time, Coke was spilling on my brand-

CHINA *Everything Is Preordained*

new Ford Probe carpeting—what a bitch!—little Joanie was in her grandpa's boat, slamming her brother over the head with her lunch bucket, in her ROTC uniform saying good-bye in Spanish to Momma and Stepmomma, then Momma bounding forward with a big, white kiss—the airbag deploying.

There was dust everywhere and a trickling sound; I figured the car was about to blow up any second so I should do what I could to get my ass out of it. The impact had jammed the doors from within, though, and I sat there stuck until this guy who saw the whole thing from behind me pulled over, pried open my door, and helped me out. I'm holding this guy who saved me while he's dialing 911.

"You okay?" he asks me.

"I think so . . ."

"Good. I gotta go. Bye!"

"Wait! Wait, please don't go, don't leave me! It wasn't my fault, it wasn't my fault!" I'm crying, clinging to him, until I could smell the bourbon on him. He had to bail, pronto, because *he* was drunk. I looked at my car and the front end was gone. A woman was hanging out of the front windshield of the other car. It was carrying four people; two of them died. The driver, intoxicated to three times the legal limit, survived. Traffic on the causeway immediately stopped moving. Helicopters were dispatched; I suf-

CHYNA

fered a fractured ankle, a broken nose, a strained back, and facial lacerations, but because my injuries weren't life-threatening, they had me wait for the ambulance. Propped up against the side of my destroyed car, I could see good Samaritans, doing what they could for the people in the other car, and I could see the long line of snarled traffic. Some guys in a pickup truck had a cooler, cracked open some beers, and kind of made the best of it.

When it was time to go, the paramedics helped me retrieve my purse from the front seat. Draped over the steering wheel was the deflated airbag—it had a lipstick imprint on it in the shape of a kiss. I was hospitalized for four days. I never made my flight . . .

I am tempted to say that the accident out there on the causeway with the ghost rider, out there in the middle of nowhere, on this ligament of land that connects the Keys to the rest of Florida, my life changed directions. I am tempted to say that a chance catastrophe, a random act of real violence led to a life of dramatized mayhem. And that how I would fall, rise, be hurt, hurt others, win, lose, bleed, and heal from that point on would be *my* call. Of course, to do so requires proof. Follow me . . .

CHINA *Everything Is Preordained*

2

Family Is Everything

REPORTER: So, your father was never welcome.

JOANIE LAURER: I don't remember my mother saying anything nice about my father.

REPORTER: And your grandparents hated him, too?

JOANIE LAURER: Right.

REPORTER: How often do you have to do your hair?

Vincent K. McMahon is my father.

Not really. Well, stepfather. Not legally. How shall I put this? Ah. Vincent K. McMahon is my StairMaster Stepfather, like it or not. (Some days I like it, some days I want to run to the nearest Club Med orphanage and steam-clean the idea.) Vince McMahon did more for me than my biological father and all three of my marginally legal step-fathers put together. Vince has other names—the Charlemagne of Pain, the Monarch of the Mat, the Titan of Tights, the Stalin of . . . well, you get the idea. I've had other names, too: Joanie, Joanie Lee, Joanie Laurer, Joanie Von Laurer, YOU MISERABLE DYKE!—again, you get the picture. Vince and I have a lot in common. He turned his daughter into a villainous, conniving bitch, his wife into a meddlesome shrew, his son into the cowardly lion, himself into a blathering, pompous stuffed pigeon, all for fun. My folks did the same to me and my brother and sister, all

CHYNA

for . . . well, "fun" is not exactly the word I would use here. I love Vince because Vince, like me, knows the meaning of dysfunction. But Vince, unlike me, doesn't take it seriously.

"When you have a variety show, which is really what we do," I heard him once say to a journalist, "sometimes the logic of the writing takes you into more soap opera than action adventure, sometimes it's more Comedy Central. It all depends which performers are being featured. The people come for many, many reasons, and one of the reasons we're successful is because we explore all of those reasons. And we try and make it so the audience never really knows what's coming; when the audience is kept off-guard and doesn't know how much of any one element they're gonna receive that night—I think that's kind of cool." As for using his family as an open book, Vince McMahon feels nothing but delight. And with the exception of the story line involving my boyfriend and the admittedly more conventionally attractive Stephanie McMahon (I think you understand where I'm coming from), I get as much a kick out of their family shenanigans as I develop a stutter talking about my own.

"Are you kidding? One of the most wonderful things that's happened to me," Vince will tell you, straight up, scout's honor, "is having my children work with me. As a parent, you simply want the best for your children. You

Family Is Everything

want them to be happy and loved. All this sounds corny, but whatever they chose to do in life, my wife, Linda, and I would've supported. Contrary to the domineering figure I play on TV, really, I'm a very sensitive individual with my own set of values. They're probably different than most everybody else's, but they work for me."

Contrary to the pile-driving, spinal-tapping, Amazonian figure I play on TV, I'm really a very sensitive, fragile little music box playing the theme song from *Titanic*. And my family? Let's see . . . that would be my biological mother, Janet, biological father, Joe, big brother, Sonny (now thirty-five), and big sister, Kathy (thirty-six), stepfather Paul, stepfather George, stepfather who-the-fuck-cares, and stepmother, Tina. To say our family values were "somewhat different" from most everybody else's is like saying Pamplona is a great place to jog. And as for whether or not our family values worked for us—hmmm. That's a tough one. Would you use the space shuttle to run up the street for a quart of milk?

I mean, if you were in a real hurry, I guess . . . huh?

Family is everything. I say that and I don't know if I should shit or wind my wristwatch. Because my family *was* everything. In the sense that, yeah, I wouldn't be who I am if Mom hadn't thrown a plate of spaghetti, if Kathy didn't punch Mom for waling on me, if Sonny didn't force me to wrestle with him in dogshit, if steppop #1 hadn't threatened

CHYNA

suicide with a shotgun, if I hadn't walked in on steppop #2 and Mom doing their thing, if Dad hadn't stabbed Mom in the thigh with a bread knife (though I don't know if it was intentional), dragged me all over the world while he tried to teach people how to shelter their money (I don't think the shelters were exactly grade A), and taken out a bunch of student loans without telling me, leaving me with a great graduation gift: a $40,000 debt that I knew nothing about.

Yeah, family is everything. Imagine your worst childhood experiences. Some of you, I'm sure, can top me, no sweat. Everybody has a sad tale. For me, it's not how bad or how awful those experiences were that makes it hard to talk about them. It's the very idea of those experiences receiving any credit for the good fortune I have at the moment. It's the *acknowledgment* that hurts. So be it. That's one of the good things about wrestling—you learn how to take a hard fall . . .

■ ■ ■

I'll make this brief. These things happened on December 27: The National Institute of Child Health and Human Development announced that it was spending one million dollars to find a cure for the listless child. A 727 jet bound for Chicago was hijacked from La Guardia and flown to Cuba. The Genesco Company came out with an innovative form of lightweight leather to be used in fashion apparel. U.S. postal workers received a 6 percent raise. Florida beat

CHINA *Family Is Everything*

North Carolina 14 to 7 in the Gator Bowl. Dow Chemical announced a significant raise in antifreeze prices. Shocking Blue's "Venus" was the number one single. The American Association for the Advancement of Science held its 134th meeting at the Sheraton Plaza Hotel in Tucson, Arizona (yes, I've stayed there!), and declared scientific investigation of UFOs inadequate. *Rolling Stone* announced the breakup of the super group Blind Faith. The *Casper* cartoon show aired its last original episode. And on that same Saturday morning, Joan Marie Laurer was born in Rochester, New York. By the way, Louis Pasteur was also born on December 27, in 1822, which may account for my obsession with germs. (When I travel I bring my own Lysol. People make fun of that sometimes. But then, they've probably never stayed in a hotel anywhere in Iowa.)

My parents, being children of the sixties, had that kind of "go with it" mentality, which was really a euphemism for being chronically irresponsible. Dad couldn't keep a job, and Mom, it turned out, couldn't keep a husband. By the time I was three, Joe and Janet had had their Spaghetti Incident (my mother dumped a plate of it over his head; he stabbed her in the thigh. Shit happens, al dente) and divorced. "Alas, we married much too young," he blithely told a reporter. In his defense, Dad was not a violent man, but he did have a problem with booze when we were kids

CHYNA

and could get ugly and stupid. Shaking a bread knife at her to make a point while he was drunkenly making himself a sandwich, he accidentally stabbed my mother in the thigh. There were times when he was so drunk he brought women home, completely forgetting that he was married. And once he allegedly fed me sewing needles as a snack. Looking back on the incident, and knowing my father, I honestly believe he didn't realize he was feeding me needles. Bringing the women home and being so drunk he didn't know he was married? Uh, that sounds like vintage Joe to me: while he was rubbing one leg (the girlfriend's), he was pulling another (my mother's).

Rochester is the corporate home of the Kodak company, and for the last half-century nearly everyone from the city either worked or had a relative who worked for the corporation. But to my dad's credit, he later got help, and when I moved in with him he was dry. My mother worked for Kodak, just as her father and mother had; so did George Ostrander, who would become my stepfather while the ink was still wet on Joe and Janet's divorce papers. (My poor brother, Sonny, by the way, still retains the unfortunate Ostrander last name.) As luck would have it, we moved (George and my mother were both transferred to Kodak's Denver offices). A few years later, Mom got sick of looking at our backyard. It was mostly dirt, some of which I ate. I got worms, and we moved. Not long

CHYNA

after returning to the Northeast, my mother got tired of looking at George. Their marriage ended with him threatening to commit suicide if my mother left him; she did, he lived, and along came Paul La Que, next in line to hold the interdomestic title of stepdad. You want a snapshot, it went like this: from 1973 to 1983 (I call it the Mommy Dearest decade) we moved a lot and most of the time my mother was angry, in love, or both. I will not even begin to try and psychoanalyze Janet Laurer or her marital problems for two reasons: First of all, when it was all going down I was too young to understand her feelings or what she was going through; and second of all, it won't change the grim truth that Sonny, Kathy, and I all suffered significantly because of it.

I could appoint myself commissioner of the Laurer World Wrestling League and unfairly match my mother's actions (she routinely withheld affection, was suspicious of everyone, and had a wicked backhand) against her virtues (she knew how to sew). I could hold my own war crimes trial, bring in witnesses, exhume dead feelings. She would testify, and not without some truth, that she did what she could to provide for us; we vacillated between white trash (the George years) and new money (Paul was a Dick years). I will respectfully counter by telling the court that this poor, misguided woman's real action against me was forgetting what it was like to be a young girl growing up, feeling awk-

CHINA *Family Is Everything*

ward, having normal insecurities, hang-ups, and fears. And then making it all worse by ignoring the fact that I was physically different. Granted, nobody has a perfect childhood and, like I said, for every rotten, scary, insane Kodak moment I had, there are other people who've had two. So. You want to know if any or all of the bullshit I went through turned Joanie into Chyna, right? Sure, sure, I grew out of the ground like a weed you couldn't kill, a big ole sunflower with triceps, and I turned to the light. Ladies and gentlemen, you were the light, and God help us all.

Well, yeah, maybe. But if I had to pick a moment from my adolescence that would most explain why I became a WWF superstar without me having to recite the Bill of Rights, light candles, and play Gloria Gaynor songs, I'd go back to seventh grade. We were living in Penfield, New York—this was after we moved back from the ill-fated sojourn in Denver. Mom was still working for Kodak and stepfather George was a mechanic. We had one of those *Brady Bunch* split levels, but that's where the similarity ends. They had a maid, we had a crabapple tree. *The Brady Bunch* was all about Mom, Dad, and apple pie. The Laurer family was all about *where* Mom was, *who* the of-the-moment fake Dad was, and real Dad's pie in the sky ("Kids. We're going to teach democracy to the Eastern Europeans!" Real quote, I swear.) But back to seventh grade . . .

CHYNA *Family Is Everything*

"Joanie, check it out—Mom just brought home a stereo," Sonny said as he came into my room one day. I was so jazzed I nearly hyperventilated. To Sonny it might as well have been a roll of toilet paper. Couple things about Sonny. First of all, he never got worked up about anything. I was a tidal wave, Kathy was a breaker, and Sonny, well, if Sonny was water, you could skip stones over him. He always smelled like airplane glue because he was into models. And he looked exactly like my dad. Which meant that if you gave him a dollar for every time my mother said to him, "You're just like your father," he could've bought enough glue to build a life-size replica of the Concorde. By the way, his real name is also Joe Laurer. (He was screwed!)

But we had our first stereo—the first one that mattered to me, anyway—and I took a header down the stairs I was so excited. Picking myself up off the floor, I saw my mother, smiling, gesturing with her hands as if she were doing her best Paula Parkinson on *The New Price Is Right,* showing the audience a Frigidaire with an ice maker. The key word there is "frigid."

"What's a matter, you don't like it?" My mother suddenly glared.

"No, no, it's—"

"Because I can take it *right* back to Sears—"

CHYNA

"Don't do that . . ." I was pleading now, my voice going shrill.

"She fell down the stairs, Ma. She loves it." Sonny tried to settle her down. That was the other thing about Sonny. My sister, Kathy, went toe-to-toe with Janet, she just wouldn't take any guff from her. Kathy *engaged,* as Captain Picard would say. Kathy taunted her. Sonny was like the steers they use to calm down the bulls they use in bullfights. He tried to nudge her away from her inclination to anger and, on more than one occasion, bore the brunt of it. Man, he tasted the lash.

"If you don't want it, I'll use it," Mom rolled on. She used this line of reasoning more than once; it was like her MO. As if she wasn't too proud to take advantage of something useful. She liked to think of herself as the kind of person who adapted, went around the tough obstacles instead of through them. Yeah, sure. (This woman was the Pythagoras of confrontation.)

But in the end, I used the stereo, I used the stereo the most out of everyone and, at the time, I thought it was the coolest thing in the house. It was a cheap piece of crap really, it would wind up in someone's yard sale long before its warranty expired. But it had detachable speakers with a lot of cord for each. I used to lie between them and crank

CHYNA

up Rick James, Culture Club, Duran Duran, and all the K-tel favorites until my balance was impaired.

Around the time that boys were wearing skinny ties to school and all the girls had their eyes made up like Joan Jett, I came home from school after a particularly rough day. There was this guy, really funny, great sense of humor,

CHINA *Family Is Everything*

smart, who helped me with this tough course that I was just stinking up the place in. And he was tall, like me. We'd spend time after school together studying, yukking it up, getting down with Fruit Roll-Ups, having a great time. Until that particular day—that's when he finally made the big pass and kissed me. And, don't get me wrong, it was a good kiss. It's just that, well, he was one of my teachers, so I sort of broke up with him. If you could really call it that.

"You have to know," this teacher says to me after the kiss—which was on the lips. Long. "I've only fallen in love with one of my students before you." Now here's a guy who just might've overthought the whole thing. Did he figure telling me that it only happened once before was, like, flattering to me? Because it sure as hell wasn't. It kind of made me feel, well, ordinary. Or did he think that confessing to me about the other student would make me trust him more? Because it sure as hell didn't. In fact, given my pre-pubescent worldview, it made me think, "Wait a minute there, Joanie—maybe this guy gets off on the, er, younger set." I had been to his house for bake-in-the-bag pork chops, met his wife and his daughter, and then he has to go and kiss me. When he could see I wasn't cool with it, he apologized, made some noise about trouble with his wife, some noise about me being irresistible, then the big grand finale about it only happening once before and that was

CHYNA

that. Looking back on it, the airbag on the causeway looks more attractive. I got a C in his class.

I was all wigged out, tense, freaked, and I needed a release. So I ran home, put on the Hall and Oates album with "Maneater," twisted that volume knob way right, and danced by myself. You know that line, "Oh, oh, here she comes—watch out"? I accidentally kicked the stereo right there, right at frigging "Watch out," and put a gouge deeper than that line on James Woods's face into the record. But worse, I knocked the dust cover off the stereo—for good. The hinge broke away from the plastic. I'm catatonic, staring at the ruined dust cover, the record's skipping, *watcha-watcha-watcha-watcha-watcha,* and, assuming she doesn't meet another potential husband on the way, Mom's due home from work. I put the broken dust cover back—it took three or four tries to get it to balance just right. If somebody the next block over so much as stifled a sneeze, that cover was on the floor again.

I went up to my room, left the door open because she had her own little after-work routine that would involve the stereo. After that, there'd be a front-and-center, then some terrible endgame. Heard the front door open. Heard my mother padding across the living room. Heard her humming (which usually meant George wouldn't be home for dinner; she liked that. To her, George was a former has-

CHINA *Family Is Everything*

been). Next thing I heard was the cheap clatter of hollow plastic bouncing on the floor, then: "WHO BROKE MY STEREO???!!"

My brother poked his innocent head in my room. "Mom wants us downstairs."

I would like to say she lined us up, *Great Santini*–style, with our nipples wired to a 6-volt battery and our feet in a tub of water, with her at the switch. But she didn't, which was too bad, because torture probably would've worked on me and I would've cracked. Instead, she made us sit in the living room.

"The three of you are gonna sit there and no one's gonna move until one of you tells me who did this," my mother swore, "and you're not gonna eat, you're not gonna watch TV, you're not gonna read, go out, talk to each other, talk to yourselves—nothing, you hear me? NOTHING, until someone tells the truth!" Then she disappeared into the kitchen. And we could hear her on the phone, speaking clearly, *sweetly*, to a friend, just making idle conversation in a way that was truly disturbing. I mean, she went from zero to sixty at warp speed. We heard other sounds, too. We could hear dishes clattering in the fridge, pouring sounds, self-satisfied sighing, as if she had Henry the Fucking Eighth in there with her and they were sharing a rotisserie chicken.

CHYNA

Dusk. We're still sitting there. She had come in once, about a half-hour earlier, to taunt us. Taunting was big with my mother. "Anybody ready to talk?" she asked. I shook my head, terrified. Sonny just hung his. Kathy wouldn't even look at her, and when Mom turned and walked out, Kathy bugged her eyes out at her behind her back. Night came. Around ten, she came in, went around the room, but didn't ask this time. Just looked at each one of us. Now, I'm a puddle of cowardice. You could wear me if you needed something yellow. And then my mother did the ultimate, worst, be-all end-all act of child abuse any of us would care to endure: She sat down in the living room with us.

Nothing like quality time to break down a suspect. So she sat there, doing that Liz Taylor thing with her knee and her foot, you know, swinging one leg in time over the other like a nutcracker. Didn't say boo. Just let us take in the

CHINA *Family Is Everything*

44

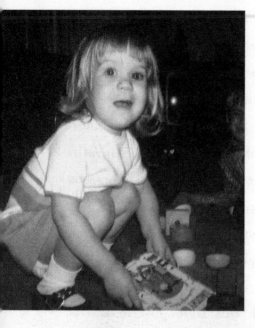

sight of her and try—go ahead, just try—to look through her, to pretend like she wasn't there. Two of us were running in opposite directions: I was melting and Kathy was hardening. And I could see the transformation in my sister. She was calling up the troops inside, she was doing a mental war dance. If she didn't out-and-out attack and strangle my mother with her bare hands, she would slap a silent treatment and an emotional embargo on this woman that would last well into the next decade. And that alone scared me, maybe as much as anything, because I wanted a family that got along, I wanted harmony. Or at least wanted to believe the rumor that it existed somewhere. I could feel the will bleeding out of me, I could feel my mom and all that she misrepresented in the way of motherhood working that submission hold on me. The thing about Jan Laurer at that time was she had all the horsepower. Whenever I went up against her, which was almost never, I could feel her gaining on me, and it was always just a matter of time before she'd catch or overcome me. And as a kid? It was actually thrilling sometimes. I could feel her

CHYNA

speed, feel how much stronger, faster, more aggressive she was than me. It was thrilling, briefly . . . then I was dead. You could apply this feeling to fighting, wrestling, sports, love, with the same depressing results. This woman was the Flo Jo of negative energy.

So she sat there, with us, and I could feel her sucking the life out of the room. I felt hot and prickly and out of breath. I could feel my mouth forming into the word "I," and if I didn't confess right then and there I was gonna suffocate—

"I did it." Sonny spoke before me. "I broke it by accident."

CHINA *Family Is Everything*

And there it was—the typical me in the typical milk shake of shame mixed with relief. The sin wasn't breaking the stereo; it probably wasn't even the not-telling part. The sin was letting somebody else take the fall instead of stepping up, taking my lumps—standing tall. Soon as I could do that, I'd have it licked. Easier said than done.

Well, Mom disappeared, left us there, just looking at each other. Then we heard plastic smashing. Like I said, Sonny liked to build models. Mom was up in his room destroying toy bombers, Corvettes, tanks, Swamp Things— everything. Then she went out somewhere to cool off. So Sonny took the shit again, took it impassively, like he always did. There was a time I recall, maybe a year before the stereo incident, when Sonny did something wrong—wrong in my mother's eyes—and she just wailed on him. Hit him high and hard, slapped the living daylights out of him. And Sonny had to be a whole head taller than my mother, too. I mean she had to nearly jump up to hit him.

"How come you just stand there and take it like that?" I asked him later. He thought about it for a second, his cheek glowing like a bee sting.

He shrugged. "I guess because it doesn't hurt. I won't let it hurt."

CHYNA

3

Choose Your Role Models with Care

People are strange when you're a
stranger. People are even more strange when you're a stranger and they act like they know you. When it comes to fans, wrestling stars are no different from any other celebrities, really. If anything, our fans might be the most passionate and rabid of all, and most of the time I wouldn't have it any other way. Yeah, yeah, you do it for yourself. You do it for the love of the game, for the sport, for the competition, but above all, you do it for the fans. Wrestling is a spectator sport in that it's all for the spectator. Without an audience, a pro wrestling match is like ballroom dancing without the music, or it's two people who already know the ending telling a story to each other. Fans make it worth doing, fans make it worthwhile. Fans give us a reason to live, fans give us everything—good fans do that. The few bad ones, though, make you want to lock yourself in a bomb shelter and sleep with a bazooka under your pillow. And I'm not talking about the fans who openly jeer and hate your character. That's totally cool, as long as they keep the throwing of bodily fluids to a minimum and remember that the Chyna who plays Hacky Sack with Val Venus's scrotum is not the Joanie who slices her bagels the same way everyone else does. I mean the bad fans who stalk you and want to get close to you to feed off of your success and your notoriety.

Bad fans have one thing in mind — themselves. And there's only one thing worse than a bad fan: *Daddy!*

About a year ago, the WWF did a show, I think it was a *Smackdown!* in Tallahassee, Florida. Most of the wrestlers were booked in the Doubletree, where I was, too. I had to do an interview and got back to the hotel about an hour later than the others. I walk into the lobby and the wrestler known as Bossman (great guy, a real sweetheart) comes up to me, all smiles.

"Hey, Joanie, I met your old man. Nice dude. We talked motorcycles."

"My old man? You mean . . . ?" I want to say the words "my dad," but they stutter in my mind before I can choke on saying them. What the fuck is he doing in Tallahassee?

"Your dad," Bossman says, like it's Ward Cleaver he ran into instead of the guy who hired bodyguards in Colombia, South America, so everyone would think he was some hot-shot tycoon. On his honeymoon. "Your dad was here. That guy really loves you."

I am walking, stunned, toward the elevators, trying to put it all together, when one of the receptionists behind the check-in counter calls to me: "Ms. Laurer?"

"Yes?" I answer, immediately disillusioning some poor six-year-old boy who just asked Chyna for her autograph.

Choose Your Role Models with Care

"There was a man here"—the receptionist is waving a piece of paper at me—"who left this—a Dr. Von Laurer? He says he knows you but he had to be somewhere and he'll try and come back. You just missed him by less than five minutes. Really nice guy."

While the boy with my autograph is tugging at his father's pant leg, trying to get an answer about the Laurer thing, I open the note, which reads:

Muffin. I need to see you. Will try later.

"What the fuck? Is he fucking nuts?" I dropped the note on the floor, ran up to my room, let myself in. "IS HE FUCKING NUTS!!!????" I'm talking to the lamps. I mean, it was beautiful, really, the message itself. Pure Joe. Began with *Muffin,* his nickname for me, which he never stopped calling me, not after dragging me all over the world as a social workhorse for his business deals that I could never understand, and not even after saddling me with forty thousand dollars in student loans, he still called me Muffin. "Muffin, you're so smart, you got a grant! Sign here." "Muffin, you're so smart, they gave you a scholarship! Sign here." "Follow the plan, follow the plan." (I never did get to see a copy of this "plan.") The guy was smooth, and the only big slipup I remember was

CHYNA

when he talked his way into this ultra-rich curling club, fell on the ice, and broke his nose. The note: middle sentence, complete. *I need to see you*. Made a big difference. *He needed to see me*. Last part, in that hurried military urgency, like as soon as he's done financing a giant IPO, negotiating peace talks between the Arabs and Israelis, and freeing some tourists from terrorists in the Philippines, he *will try later*. Not that I might be guilty of overthinking the whole thing. But every time the guy got in touch with me out of the blue, every time I was even remotely reminded of him in some way, I always had the same reaction. For example, in some recent magazine article about me, he is quoted as saying I will suffer deep psychological damage for not contacting him or letting him in my life. Yeah, I'll make contact. My fist and your face. Yeah, yeah, that's what I'll do. My fist. Your face. And there I was, in the Doubletree hotel, a grown woman, capable of taking complete care of herself, capable of facing anything, muttering, "Yeah, yeah, that's the ticket. My fist. Your face. You better hope I don't see you before you see me." He never showed up. And if he would've, I probably wouldn't have clobbered him. He's my biggest fan . . . right? As for deep psychological damage, by the time I showed up at age sixteen, on his doorstep, that had been handily taken care of.

CHYNA *Choose Your Role Models with Care*

November 1983 By now you may have guessed that as a teenager, living with my mother was pretty damn fucked up. She had rules that changed with her moods and husbands that changed with even less predictability. I had rules, too, which I set myself. Since I had been surrounded by these rules most of my adolescent life, I was determined not to end up a loser. Losers got bad grades, struggled, and ended up homeless or deluded, like my mother. Losers became drunks or took lots and lots of drugs and became addicted, struggled, and ended up homeless or deluded, like my father. Although at the time I had no fucking idea how really deluded he was. In fact, at the time, *I* was the one who was deluded because he was my hero.

Sophomore year at Pittsford Sutherland High was probably the height of my dark ages. While I did good schoolwork and got good grades, I had slipped into this kind of path-of-least-resistance way of life, which involved lying, purging, and getting away with shit without getting caught. Hey, like the saying goes, the apple doesn't rot—er, fall—far from the tree. Around this time I was flirting with bulimia. I'd binge on bags of sour-cream potato skins, hit the can, tickle the ole Adam's apple, do the Technicolor yawn into the toilet, and voilà, I am thin again. I made it down to a size 4. I ran with a pretty cool crowd at school— pot smokers. I tried it two, maybe three times and didn't

CHYNA

like it, but I loved the company, in particular a girlfriend named Gena.

Gena's family had money; we had my mother's husband Paul, which put us in the demi-nouveau-riche tax bracket. We lived in a two-story colonial with wood floors, lots of bathrooms, closet space—it was pretty impressive until a train went past. The house was, at most, seventy-five yards from the tracks. I won't say the whole house rattled, but if you peed standing up and a train went by, the floor was gonna get wet. But Gena's family had real money, and since a shallow value system is better than none at all, I kind of envied Gena for being indulged, for having dough. Now, with her fifteenth birthday approaching, I was in a panic because I had no money to buy her a present. I suppose a hug or a card would've sufficed, but I wanted to impress Gena. Of course, I could sew like nobody's business, but I wanted it kept that way. There was just something a little too white trash about making her a shirt or knitting her a tube top. I mean, gimme a break, everybody'd seen *Pretty in Pink*. Gena was way too cool for arts and crafts. I remember she took me to this party when I was in seventh grade, at this chick's apartment. I can't remember exactly how Gena got to be friends with this girl—she was nineteen—but, boy, do I remember the party.

CHYNA *Choose Your Role Models with Care*

"How old are you?" Gena coached me on the way over.

"Thirteen. Just like you."

"Stop joking. This is serious. Tonight, you're sixteen. Say it."

"Tonight, I'm sixteen."

"Good." Gena gave me a stick of clove gum that she claimed would make the boys horny. (This may explain my longtime gum fetish with Hubba Bubba bubble gum. Blueberry was my favorite.) "You're sixteen. When we get to the party? I want you to act like you're two years older than *that*."

The apartment was this purple and black flophouse, a kegger in the bathtub and a poster of Frankie Goes to Hollywood over the fake fireplace. Guys everywhere, everybody making out. Now, in seventh grade I was at least five-foot-six, maybe 120 pounds, so I looked the part. All the older seductresses in *Sixteen Candles* always looked right in the dude's eyes. You know, head a little tilted up. So I did that a lot and hooked up with this really cute guy. We're sitting on a couch and he kisses me, which was cool, I guess. When we stopped kissing, I gave him the sexy *Sixteen Candles* look. He looked at me, grabbed my head, and pulled it down into his crotch. Ah, the opposite sex. I managed to wriggle free and stood in the corner for the rest of the night

CHYNA

disgusted, which was all the same, since word quickly got out that I was not into blowing guys on the first hello.

Back to Gena's birthday present. My first thought was a couple packs of clove gum, but nah, she'd laugh, then see through it—that I was cheap or didn't have any money.

"Wow, these are, like, very, very cool!" Gena was honestly, truly impressed with the earrings I decided to give her.

"They're not diamond," I told her, just to be, you know, honest. "They're zircon."

"I know," she told me, "but they're still way cool. Where'd you get them?"

A few days later, I'm in my room listening to Rick Dees on the radio, still a little disturbed that Gena knew, just by looking at them, that the earrings were zircon.

"Joanie! Get out here right now!!!" My mother is hollering somewhere in the house. Climbing out of bed, I go look for her. She had that tone like something bad happened.

"JOANIE! HURRY UP!" she hollers again, not to be found in her room, in the bathroom, or in any of the upstairs, but her voice sounds close—very, very close. I go back to her bedroom—still empty. Check the closets. "Where are you, Ma?"

"OUT HERE!" she calls, and it sounds like her voice is coming from, well, the roof. Sure enough, I put my head out of her bedroom window. And she was on the roof. On her knees, *pointing*.

"What're you doing, Mom?"

"You see them?"

"See what? Shingles?"

"Very funny. FOOTPRINTS. Look. Look at the marks. They're footprints. I think they're Sonny's," she snarled, rubbing the dirt off her hands. She had thrown Sonny out of the house a few years back.

"Why would Sonny's footprints be on the roof?"

"He snuck in the house, that's why. You see them? You do see them?"

I did, as a matter of fact. There were definitely footprints on the roof. They could've been old footprints, which I suggested and immediately regretted because she hollered, "THOSE ARE NEW FOOTPRINTS!" so loudly she nearly fell off the roof herself. When I got her back inside she was already suspecting ex-husband George faster than you can say "zircon": "George snuck in and took my earrings!"

Wouldn't you know it. She never, ever, wore those earrings, just let them collect dust in her jewelry box. I pinch them and alarms go off—I mean, the woman had a sixth sense. And after she discovered them missing I walked around the house for almost a week freaked out and won-

CHYNA

dering when she'd finally get around to accusing me. One day Gena showed up at the house—wearing the earrings. Now there was an afternoon to remember. She's gonna see them, she's gonna beat the crap out of me, and I'm gonna get kicked out of the house. I couldn't tell Gena to take them off—that would've been humiliating. And I sure as hell wasn't going to tell my mother, because knowing her, she would've demanded them back from Gena, and that would've been humiliation cubed. So I just let it ride. As it turned out, my mother never even noticed the earrings on her. Still, these were not fun times.

To calm myself, I ate lots and lots of food, stuck my arm down my throat, hit the bathroom tiles, and drove the big white porcelain bus. Vomiting until my stomach lining started showing up in the toilet, I broke blood vessels in my eyes, developed spider veins. I looked like shit because I wasn't gaining any weight. I was always a little withdrawn, right? Well, at that time, I was quiet as a church mouse. And Mom got suspicious.

"We're all going for a ride," she said some days later, "you, me, and Paul," and she wasn't asking, she made that clear.

"Okay. Where?" I asked.

Just for a ride, I was told. But looking out my window, I saw the sign as we slowed, pulled into the parking lot. My breath smelled like spoiled taco meat.

CHYNA

We went straight to some drug-rehab center. On the way over, Mom aired her suspicion—that I was getting high, which I denied. I told her I tried it a few times, hated it, that it was for losers, all to no avail because she had gone in my room, found notes that Gena wrote to me about how high she was at this party or in school. And it didn't matter that Gena wrote the letters or that Gena was the one talking about getting high. It was pure guilt by association. You know how you see yourself walking into or toward something completely awful? And you have a chance to run, to get away, to put up a fight, but your curiosity gets the better of you? That's what this was like.

I walk in, pass this recreational room. Kids slouching everywhere in concert T-shirts, their hair fried orange, the TV on. It was my worst *loser* nightmare come to life. This guy who works for the center, some smiling dude in a sweatsuit and hard shoes with his wallet chained to his pants, directs me into a waiting room. I sit there alone for a while (companionship vs. solitary—big weapon). I guess they wanted to make me sweat, to soften me up the way you marinate chicken. Finally, this counselor comes in, woman, mid-thirties, and she's got the unisex hair and the tough-love thing working overtime, like she's seen all of Tyne Daly's work. I mean, maybe it was me, maybe I came off as resentful and stubborn, but I was innocent and this was

Choose Your
Role Models with Care

insane. And besides, this woman seemed as if she'd seen and heard it all anyway, and what I had to say mattered little. Eventually, they'd get to the bottom of it, whatever it was.

"Do you take drugs?" Tyne Daly asked.

"No."

"Have you tried drugs?"

"Yes."

"Then you *do* take drugs."

"I tried pot a few times and didn't like it."

"Do you take pills?"

"No."

"Do you drink alcohol?"

"No, but—"

"—you tried it a few times."

"Once. Yeah. In eighth grade. I had four beers at a Deep Purple concert, puked my guts out, and never touched the stuff again." This was true. Kathy took me, we had a blast, and I won the Olympic cookie toss. They sold tons of T-shirts that night due to the unexpected stains on the clothing of people sitting nearby.

Eventually, the woman stopped asking questions and silently reviewed my responses, which she had written down. Then she opened a cabinet door, found one of those little frosted plastic cups, handed it to me, and although there was no need to explain, she said, "We need some of your urine."

Peeing. Yeah, I've tried that a few times and actually liked it. So they took my urine, tested it for drugs. It came back negative, but that didn't stop Tyne Daly. She told me kids routinely do things to cover up the presence of drugs in their system. Yeah, I'm sure that's true. But this was a sneak attack, I countered. I didn't even know I was coming here. Unless she thought that on the way to the bathroom, I made instant friends with one of those burned-out kids in the rec room and one of them sold me some piss contraband. Then she argued that sometimes the drugs don't show up in the test and from there, leapfrogged into a whole impassioned speech about denial, how I was in serious denial, that I had a problem, and, oh, yeah, that I'd been "treating some people badly in my life." But all of that could be addressed and taken care of if I would allow myself to be treated. I said no. That was it. End of story. No. N-O. No and hell-no.

"You're going into that drug-rehab center," my mother threatened me when we got home. "YOU WILL GO THERE OR YOU WILL LEAVE THIS HOUSE." Looking back on it, I think she may have really thought that I had some kind of a problem, whether it was drugs or with her or with myself. And, frankly, I think she could've been convinced that the drug-rehab place just wasn't the answer. But you don't stare down my mom; she doesn't

*Choose Your
Role Models with Care*

blink. The biggest reason she gave me that ultimatum? The biggest reason she wanted me to go into the drug-rehab center was because I didn't want to go.

Toothbrush: check. Platforms: check. Pat Benatar cassette: check. Paperback of classic Winnie the Pooh stories: check. Broken fucking heart: check. Packed a few double-thickness grocery bags with some clothes and I walked out of the house for good. On the porch, my mother stood in Paul's arms and cried, going back and forth from "How could you do this to your own mother?" to "You leave and you'll never set foot in this house again!"

I spent two weeks in a sort of limbo, stayed at Gena's house, slept in her room on the floor. And it took a while to get to sleep because I had to fight off this terrible loneliness and abandonment. The room vibrated in the dark with it. Yeah, okay, I chose to leave, I made my bed and now I'm lying on the floor in it. But I'm barely sixteen. And in order to cope with being alone, I schemed. I tried to think of the one thing that would put a dagger in my mother's back for what she did.

"Uh . . . hello? Is this the Joe Laurer residence?" I asked the man on the phone.

"Yes, it is," the man pleasantly answered. He sounded kind of old.

"I'm trying to find my dad—he's Joe Laurer. This is his daughter Joanie . . ."

CHYNA

"Joanie! My God, little Joanie! This is Gramps! You called Joe Senior! Let me give you your dad's number. My goodness, he's going to be so happy to hear from you!"

Well, I finally called my dad and Gramps was right; my dad was so happy to hear from me that I felt like some chosen little Buddha. You'd think he'd been looking for me all his adult life and finally found me. Ten minutes into the conversation he asked me to move in with him.

"You're going to be with me, now, Joanie. And I'm going to take care of you," he gushed. I had no reason to doubt him.

Meet Joe Laurer. Six feet, Wile E. Coyote build, voice like Mr. Rogers on speed. He was unreal. Maybe that's why I liked him so much. You could stomp on him, you could beat him, catch him red-handed. You could dismiss him, divorce him, take his money (which was probably yours to begin with), call his bluff. His eyes might glaze for a brief second, but then he'd shake it off and sing "Life is a cabaret" out of his ass. He never stopped maintaining his innocence. Not actual, real innocence—he knew he could charm fleas off a dog—but in spirit. His mantra was "Who, *me*?" Nobody said it better. And the guy knew how to have fun. If he wanted to, he could probably have left a path of financial ruin across three continents, but he sure knew how to have fun.

My mother, of course, was livid. She'd call, demanding

that I come home. This was after she had flung all of my belongings out of the second-story window of her house. I had to retrieve them while all the nosy neighbors gawked at the Laurer sideshow. She'd call the police, report that I was being held against my will, but through it all my dad was blithe and unflappable. My mother called the second day I was there; my dad and I picked up at the same time, but I let him talk—neither of them knew I was on the line.

"Where's Joanie?" she demanded.

"Now, Jan, calm yourself down. She's here, she's just fine. Would you like to talk to her?"

"You're damn right I want to talk to her! Now, put her on!!!"

Dad set down the phone and literally sang, "Joanieeeee, your mother's on the phone!"

I pretended to pick up, tried doing the singsong thing, like, gee, long time no hear.

"How could you do this to me?" she hissed. "This is the worst thing you could do! How could you end up with that man?? Do you know what he did to me? You are so ungrateful! You're staying with a man who tortured me!"

And now, a few words from the loyal opposition (Joe Laurer, to a reporter, 2/17/00):

CHYNA

Joanie's mother and I didn't get along very well. Jan was my high school sweetheart. We met in the high school orchestra. Jan played first cello and I played the violin and later the string bass. We traveled all over New York together as part of the inter–high school orchestra. She was the apple of my eye. After high school, I joined the army and I began to dream about her, so we started to correspond every day. Just before shipping over to Italy, we eloped. We found a justice of the peace in Rochester, paid him ten dollars in dimes, then borrowed money from my parents for a motel room. It was something out of a storybook. However, we were too young, and when Joanie was about four, we were divorced.

"And later the string bass?" Okay, so he tortured her, that's obvious. But I was also staying with a man who structured his days around errands that we could do together. First there was breakfast at Harriet's, then on to the post office, then a stop at Kmart, and, finally, we'd go to the Publix supermarket to pick up that night's dinner. This was our itinerary just about every day. I was living with a man who remarried a younger woman named Tina, who was almost

as much fun as he was. I was living with a man who just flattered the hell out of me: "Joanie, you are going to become a foreign diplomat! I can feel it," or "Joanie, I've got great plans for you, but anything you choose to do you will succeed in." And in his own way, during that first year with him, he did everything for me. I say "in his own way" because it was like being spoiled by Gomez Addams.

Like when I turned sixteen and got my driver's license. A few months after I passed the test, my dad picked me up from school. He's got this big, cat-who-swallowed-the-canary smile on his face. "I have a surprise for you," he says, then drives me to this heavily industrialized part of Rochester, over on Culver Road. Stops the car in front of an auto-repair joint in a building that used to be some kind of a foundry. You could scratch your name out in the caked grease on the floor. Dad walks me up to one of the cars crouched near the front—a Chevette painted the color of dirty paper money. There's a shock coat of primer on one door to cover some messenger-service emblem. Dad jams his hand down into his pockets, comes up with a set of keys, and points to the Chevette.

"It's all yours!" he says, giving me a great smile. And I am beside myself with joy. My own car! My own preowned, fully unloaded Chevette! I climbed in, adjusted the rearview mir-

CHYNA

rors, honked the horn (it didn't honk), tried the wipers (passengers would see clearly in the rain, but the driver's-side wiper was shredded like a violin bow after a Charlie Daniels concert). But it had a cool phony leather steering wheel and an AM/FM radio and, uh-oh—a stick shift.

"Uh, Dad, this is a manual transmission—I can't drive stick."

"Sure, you can, Muffin. It's easy, you'll figure it out. Bye." He kissed me on the cheek and he ambled off.

"No, wait! I can't drive this car!"

"Make an H with your fist," he said over his shoulder. I wanted to make something else with my fist, but he was already driving off. In his own way he was trying to teach me to be independent, but it's as if the guy walked up to the dysfunctional window and said, supersize me! I saw what he meant by the H—it was right there on the stick-shift knob—and I practiced dumping the clutch a few times. Seemed easy enough—until I actually started the car in first gear while pumping the gas. The Chevette did this ghetto bounce out into the middle of the busiest street in Rochester, the whole transmission howling in pain, then the engine died. Suddenly I am everybody's commuter nightmare, the idiot who not only snarls traffic but does so while she's moving. I could drive for fifty feet before the

Choose Your
Role Models with Care

car lurched to a stop from too much gas or from too much clutch or making a K instead of an H with the stick shift. It was like being on a pair of two-thousand-pound roller skates for the first time, but I finally made it home.

Now, you have to remember that at the time, to me, Joe Laurer (there's a better than even chance that he was *tri-polar*) was my savior. He got me out of my mother's place and gave me a Chevette. Walking into the living room a little unnerved, I saw him sitting there, looking positively saintly, glasses on the tip of his nose, wearing a buttoned-up sweater and reading some book about how to make a fortune growing basil or something. Before I can recount to him how I nearly became the human filling in a scrap-iron Chevette cookie, he casually calls over his shoulder, "Oh, there you are, Muffin. I was beginning to worry."

"Yeah, well, it took me a little longer than I expected to learn to use a clutch and a stick shift and a gas pedal and a brake in the middle of rush-hour traffic, you know?"

"So you got the hang of it, then! Great! Listen, run up to the store and get me a carton of cigarettes, okay? Chop chop. I have two more chapters here."

The store he was talking about was on Mount Hope Avenue. Now, d'you ever wonder why they name a street Elm Street, but there's not a single elm anywhere? Or, like,

CHYNA

Castle Street, and you see nothing but mobile homes? Well, there's a real good reason why Mount Hope Avenue is not just Hope Avenue. It's a hill, a big, big hill, and at the top of the hill you'll find a grocery store. For someone who just learned how to drive stick, that wouldn't be too bad as long as you didn't have to stop at a stoplight halfway to the top. Joe Laurer's unintentional lessons in life, number 43: If you don't keep going forward, you'll roll backward and crash. And if you stay where you are, you'll never get cigarettes.

CHYNA *Choose Your Role Models with Care*

4

Nobody Gets Hurt

My tit aches. Hunter could barely

get out of bed this morning—his back and legs were stiff. And last night, I swear, Sean Michaels would've looked like a walking ad for a hospital-supply outfit—if he could've walked. The cartilage in his knees is gone; an X ray of his spine would look like the Colorado River. And me, my tit is killing me. Chris Benoit put the cross-face Crippler on me and damn, he is gentle. It looks like he's turning my head into a giant Chyna Pez dispenser, but that's not what put the hurt on the ole sweater puppies. See, when Chris let me up, Eddie inadvertently tripped on the ref's arm, and his boot caught me just as I was rolling over. And it probably wouldn't have hurt at all, but I have some scar tissue from a previous injury and once in a while it flares up. It all began with my breast implants a few years ago.

"Oh, you have such gorgeous breasts," the journalist E. G. Carol remarked during an interview not long ago.

"Well, she oughta," Hunter groused. "She paid enough for 'em. TWICE." Well said.

When things began to pop for me, so to speak, I decided to add a little something to the total package. Now, I already had the muscles, the toning, and a fat-to-body-weight ratio to freakin' die for, if I say so myself. And I loved all of that, I loved being big and strong and powerful—and that was nonnegotiable. I would never give up my

CHYNA

muscles. I have designs on acting; I've done bit parts on sit-coms and TV dramas. Not long ago, a journalist buddy of mine asked me this: If I was offered an incredible Meryl Streep–Michelle Pfeiffer–type role, just a great, complex role in a film, but there was one condition, that I had to lose some of my muscles, would I do it? Not on your life. Not now, not never. Muscles are as much a part of me as the pores in my skin, or the blood that pumps fast in me when love comes to town. The thing I did feel I could use was a little femininity. I had it on the inside (I enjoy being a girl as much as the next gal), but I figured I could use a few more curves. I mean, why do I have to be butch? Just because I'm an ass-kicker doesn't mean I can't have a little cleavage, does it? And while we're grinding that ax, men vs. women? Are you serious? *Men vs. women?* Ha! Here's the huge double standard in a nutshell. The guys? Aside from hair—Hunter, Edge, and Christian, for example—all they have to do is look, well, manly. And that, dear, patient friends, covers a lot of ground. They can stink (Rakishi is way over with the stink face), they can sweat, they can be fat, old, small, silly. Women? Oh, boy. Terry? Lita? Steph? We all have to look enticing while getting the cellulite beaten out of us. You're expected to grimace and look gor-geous, you're supposed to pass out, land awkwardly but suggestively, you're supposed to get smashed into a folding

CHINA *Nobody Gets Hurt*

table, flipped, and thrown, then remember to land tit side up. Cameramen? You get no help from them; they've been running around for years chasing sweaty men, so what do they know about unflattering angles or harsh lights? Some of us have spent years trying to find the right makeup, the right hair to stand up under those lights and those fucking handheld cameras that are right up your ass. Clothes? Kurt Angle puts on his nursery school Olympic wrestling outfit, making sure the package is heavily outlined. Hunter, The Rock? Black leather Speedos. Done. Take me to the ring. But us? You pick something out that's black, V-cut, and you think you're showing enough breast (breasts are mandatory, in case you missed it) during the taping. But you watch it on TV when the show actually runs and it looks like you're wearing a turtleneck. Things just don't quite turn out as they seem to when you do them. A zit you thought you camouflaged looks like a fucking tumor. Makeup? It's even worse for me, because I'm in there fighting, being the heel sometimes, having my head grabbed, pinched between Big Show's thighs or locked under X-Pac's armpit. That means finding products that don't smudge. Bright red lipstick is suicide.

Seriously, I always liked the fact that I could break into the wrestling world—a man's world—without having to resort to T&A. There have been and always will be female

CHYNA

wrestlers . . . who shake their asses, bat their eyelashes, make out in the ring, do the whole Jezebel thing to entice men, then take them out with a shoe or something when they're not looking. Well, yeah, it's a story line, it's fiction. But the idea of it is that women will always have apples and men love apple pie—and not to get too heavy, but it turns women into villains. It makes sex bad. And even I know that's not true. Sex is good and a good pair of tits is golden.

Now, there are two, and only two, ways to purchase a set of tits: you can go the bargain basement route and end up with cross-eyed cleavage or you can do the research thing—research, Internet, titty-banger hot lines—and be ready to shell out some major bank. I believe I acted responsibly, as I always have with any health issue concerning my body. I believe the surgeon who gave me my implants, an extremely competent and well-respected individual in his field, acted responsibly. What neither of us counted on was the unique prototype—years of physical conditioning, bodybuilding, and strength development had created a new Joanie. And getting just the right look, the right proportion, was like trying to slap a pair of wings on a Volkswagen and calling it an airplane. Unless you make some changes to that there fuselage, the damn thing just ain't gonna fly.

I wanted breasts that would look natural. It was not my intention to transform myself into WWF Barbie, you

CHYNA *Nobody Gets Hurt*

know, with a set of hooters that defied the laws of gravity or that would guarantee buoyancy should I ever be swept away in a flood. Still, I am five-ten, so it was not unreasonable or imprudent to go with a large implant size. And, as I said, I wanted a natural look, so we went with the teardrop shape.

I recall looking in the mirror just after the procedure and being a little underwhelmed.

"Gee," I said to the doctor, "they look a lot smaller than I expected."

"You know what? I have to be honest, I think you're right, Joanie," he concurred.

The teardrops just did not look right on me. It felt like I had boobs under my armpits; not only that, it looked like I was wearing a couple of gourds on my chest because they sat on top of all that muscle. And chances are, I'd still have them if I hadn't wrestled Savio Vega five months later. Vega, bless his heart, clotheslined me during an elimination

CHYNA

match. A clothesline is a simple contact/momentum move. With your opponent coming full-bore at you, you stick out your arm, catching him—or her—in the chest and neck and violently stopping his forward momentum, with spectacular results. Picture driving a Miata underneath a semitrailer. I bounced off the ropes, catapulted into Vega, he clotheslined me just right, and for a second my chest felt like a thousand volts were coursing through it, then I was fine. Just for that one brief second when his arm caught me it burned.

That night, Hunter and I made love. He grabbed my tit and I thought he had pincers—I remember shouting, it hurt so bad, but again, the pain disappeared as fast as it came. Next morning, I'm standing naked in front of the mirror.

"Hunter, come here. Look."

"Yeah. Nice."

"No, no . . . look closely. Doesn't one look smaller than the other?"

"Nah. You're imagining it." If anything, Hunter thought one might be a little swollen from Vega's pounding. Of course, the one that Vega hit was smaller, not larger, so I called the doctor's office. I got his assistant, asked her what would happen if I punctured an implant.

"Oh, you'd know right away because it would go down

CHYNA

immediately," she insisted. They just plain pop, I was told.
Right.

We were on a two-week road trip. In Boston, I began
crabbing about the slight list to my posture. When we hit
Milwaukee, I swear my left tit was as flat as a glass of day-
old beer. By the time we rolled into Saint Louis, one side of
me looked like that arch they have there and the other side
looked like the landscape of Kansas. And that was just the
first week; we still had five dates to go before I could have

CHINA *Nobody Gets Hurt*

the thing repaired. I still had to perform and resorted to wearing vests and stuffing sweatsocks inside of my bra.

I finally got home and had a powwow with my surgeon. Since I had to go under the knife again, I decided to get bigger implants. The problem was I had already been equipped with the biggest implant available the first time around—of those that had been mass-manufactured. So my surgeon had a pair of what are now being called Chyna 2000s custom designed to fit the proportions of my size and body. Like E. G. Carol said—the breasts were gorgeous. The operation was sheer hell, and I still feel it now and then. Because I had such highly developed muscle tissue, the surgeon had to pull and pull and pull to fit the Chyna 2000s in my chest.

Being a woman and experiencing physical pain because of it is something that's shadowed me almost all my life. The connection between becoming a pro wrestler, ultimately fighting men at their own game, and the process of becoming a woman? I believe the word is "nexus." Well, that connection, that nexus just might be as close as the distance between Joanie and Chyna. All that defined me as a woman in the physical sense just plain *hurt*. It seemed to just work out that way—I mean, saying the word even hurts. I suffered becoming a woman. Maybe that's why it was so important to become strong.

■ ■ ■

CHYNA

I am sweet sixteen. I would like to add never-been-kissed, but I told you about that teacher in seventh grade, so . . .

I've been living with my father and my stepmom, Tina, for a few months now. Tina, who was nothing if not a great girlfriend to me, knew about my boyfriend, Ron, and rightly figured we were about to make a big splash sexually. She suggested some means of birth control, which meant a visit to the gynecologist.

I came out of the gynecologist's office no longer sweet sixteen but, according to the nurses, very pregnant. Now, unless it all happened while I was asleep or you can get pregnant wearing your boyfriend's cutoffs (I've done that a few times. Ron had this pair that made my ass look like Joan Jett's), there was no way that I could have a little Laurer in the oven. I mean, come on, I was a virgin. And if anyone— ANYONE—would know they had had sex or not it would be me. Let's just say I was tall enough to have a good view of it and leave it at that. After repeated pregnancy tests came back negative, the doctors did X rays and discovered a tumor the size of a grapefruit. No pain, no distended area, just a big scary ovarian tumor. The reason I never felt anything was because I had begun to work out around that time and my stomach muscles were extremely strong.

Then followed the kind of talk and conjecture that makes your neck feel like a noose is tightening around it.

CHYNA *Nobody Gets Hurt*

Naturally, I saw a half-dozen specialists, got second opinions, and spent a good deal of time in waiting rooms staring at magazines. I felt like *People*'s 50 Most Beautiful People would outlive me, fish in waiting-room aquariums would outlive me, terrible, dust-laden Norman Rockwell prints of country doctors jamming needles into little boys' asses would remain up and dusty long after I was gone. Worst of all there were nurses and receptionists who always seemed to know more about my terrible fate than I did and were dreadfully embarrassed about it because none of them would ever look me in the eye. The word "hysterectomy" came up several times; I was shown diagrams of the female reproductive system so many times that I began to draw it on my own in my classes.

"Joanie . . . what a nice steer's head. I see the Picasso influence . . ."

CHYNA

■ ■ ■

I should explain something about my relationship with my mother. Yes, I was living with my dad at the time, but my mother had a sphere of influence on me that was as big as one of Jupiter's moons. To say the word "woman" makes me wince; to say the word "mother"? Somebody get me a trash bag full of Valium. My mother could be sipping gin, marrying extraterrestrials, ruining lives in another solar system—in another *galaxy*—and I could feel her as if she were standing over my shoulder smoking a Virginia Slim. This lady had *space,* and in the emotional algebra of our lives, her circles intersected mine whether I wanted them to or not. I can honestly say that I will never be close to my mother again. Hell, I don't have to, she's right here, saying, "Joanie, don't lie, you're high on drugs; Joanie, don't lie, you had sex; Joanie, don't lie, you like your father better than me; Joanie, don't lie, you hate my boyfriend; Joanie, tell the truth . . ." Janet Laurer, then, became my Other, the Voice, the Conscience. Didn't matter that I was with Dad, who, in his own way, was much more forgiving. Here's a little something I lifted off the Internet recently, a little something my dad provided to ome journalist who was doing an unauthorized piece on me:

Joanie was a beautiful baby with curly strawberry blond hair, started walking at seven months and

HYNA

even then she had a beautiful smile. Joanie
showed signs of genius even as a diarrhea toddler.
She learned to swim at age two, was reading by
the time she was three, and had a handle on
writing long before she started school. She also
demonstrated a hearty sense of humor at an early
age, constantly making jokes, imitating television
characters, hiding things, and making faces. She
rarely cried. She was happy. We had fun together
and she was truly a treasure.

Okay, here's the thing: He knows he'll never see a dime from me; he knows that when I'm not reading *Iron John* or *Men Are from Mars, Women Are from Venus,* I fantasize punching him in the face; he knows that our chance of having a father-daughter relationship at this point is about as likely as snow falling on cedars in El Paso. Still, he said these nice things, which makes him either seriously deluded or kind of decent in his own dysfunctional way. I'll let you draw your own conclusions. "Hiding things, making faces . . ." I love that. Sounds a little like Hunter.

It stands to reason, then, that a week before my operation, I called to fill my mother in, called her because in some twisted way, I had to confess. Called her because, frankly, I was also a little scared.

CHINA *Nobody Gets Hurt*

"It's okay, okay, you're gonna do just fine," she reassured me, then added, "and for once, all your dumbbell-lifting is gonna work in your favor."

"Dumbbell . . . what? Are you—?"

"The strongest-man stuff that you do—"

"Weightlifting, Mother, I lift weights—"

"Whatever," she cut me off. "It'll help you get through the recovery process sooner. Now, I have a really excellent gynecologist I want you to see. He's not one of these quick-to-cut fellas—"

"Mom, listen—"

"I'm gonna look up his number right now."

"Mom . . ."

"No, I have it right here. Do you have a pencil? Now, don't try to remember this in your head, write it down, go and get a pencil."

"MOM. Did you hear me at all? It's set. I've been through a million tests, they know exactly what's wrong, and the operation is set for next Wednesday."

There was a silence over the phone that I could've used to shave my legs. I could feel her tighten up, feel her ire. "Fine," she snapped. "Fine. You do it your way, but don't expect any help from me, Joanie. That's it. You go do this your way, but don't come asking me for advice or help. It's your big choice and you're smarter than the rest of us anyway—"

CHINA *Nobody Gets Hurt*

CLICK. I mean, I didn't hang up on her, and she, to her credit, didn't hang up on me, but useful information and any semblance of mother-daughter kindness stopped long before we said good-bye. "Don't worry, Muffin," my dad said, after I hung up. "We'll take care of everything." Incidentally, whenever he called me "Muffin," it was usually code for trouble.

I had the surgery. Painful? They cut through your abdominal wall, and because I had such thick stomach muscles it was akin to going through a log with a rusty handsaw. I woke up after the operation and saw the staples they used to close me up. I had a zipper. The doctor had removed the tumor. Tina and my father visited once a day; my mother never called. I was hospitalized for three days, then spent about three weeks at home recuperating. There were follow-up tests. No sign of cancer. It felt like someone left a pair of cowboy spurs where the sun don't shine, but prognosis for full recovery was bright. Well, not entirely bright. About five weeks after the surgery, there were a few, um, complications.

I drove to the doctor's office for a routine follow-up, feeling good, able to use the clutch on this piece of shit Pontiac T-1000 that I was driving at the time (I tried driving a few weeks after the surgery and probably ground enough

CHYNA

metal off the transmission to fit braces on a family of ten with overbites). The doctor calls me into his office—Dr. Tichell—we're going over a few things, diet, etc., when there's a knock at the door. Nurse pokes her head in, says, "Joanie, there's someone here to see you," but before I can reply—KAPOW!!!!—the door blows open and Paul, my stepfather, comes roaring in, screaming like The Rock after he's been pantsed by Shane McMahon, Edge, and Christian, on such a tear he's spitting on the harder consonants: "HOW DID YOU DO IT, JOAN!? HUH? HOW DID YOU DO IT!?"

Dr. Tichell is astonished, and picks up his phone like he's going to dial the police. Instead he hangs it up and *he* starts hollering: "Hey! Hey! I want you out of this office, right now! You can't talk to this young woman like this! Who the hell do you think you are—"

"HOW'D YOU DO IT, JOANIE?" Paul is locked on me like a spring-loaded bear trap. I mean, it's like Dr. Tichell doesn't even exist. "WHY NOT SHOW US ALL HOW YOU DID IT, YOU LITTLE BITCH!!!"

"YOU," Dr. Tichell is pointing at Paul, "YOU LEAVE RIGHT NOW OR I'M CALLING THE POLICE!" Tichell keeps picking up the phone (hope for me!) like he's about to dial, but then thinks of something he wants to yell

and puts the phone down again (no hope for me!)—"YOU ARE *AN ANIMAL!*"

I duck under Paul's arm, run out to the elevator, jump in—he slams his arm between the doors, *Friday the 13th*–style, the doors blabbering against his arm, opening-closing until he wriggles in, corners me, starts hollering to the point where I can see the roots of his teeth growing out of his gums. "YOU THINK YOU'RE SO DAMNED CLEVER, DON'T YOU, YOU LITTLE BITCH!!" I'm crying, stumbling, trying to get free, finally breaking out from his arms, and I run out into the parking lot, lurch into my car, lock the doors, start the damned thing, grind the gears, pull out. I immediately have to slam on the brakes in order to not hit my mother's car because she's done this idiotic, showboating, *Starsky and Hutch* maneuver, cutting me off with her Mitsubishi Laser ("The headlights remind me of James Bond," she told my sister once). She slams her car into park, flings open her door, bolts up to my T-1000, and starts banging on the window, screaming, "WHY? WHY? WHY DID YOU DO THIS TO ME? YOU ARE NOT MY DAUGHTER ANYMORE, YOU HEAR ME! YOU ARE NO LONGER A MEMBER OF MY FAMILY! JOANIE! *JOANIE!*"

Now a crowd of people is beginning to form on the side-

CHYNA

walks and the next thing I know, my mother throws herself down on the hood of my Pontiac, but she can't seem to get a grip on it and rolls off, disappearing from view. I'm freaked—did she fall under the car? Did she pass out? Disappear? I climb out and find her stretched out in front of the car. Remember those protesters in Tiananmen Square, lying in front of the tanks? That's what she was doing. And she had me cornered, there was no way to back the car up without hitting another car.

"YOU'RE NOT MY DAUGHTER ANYMORE!!!!!" Flat on her back, she's roaring.

"All right, fine!! You can lay there as long as you want!! You can scream and yell as long as you want, I don't care!" I hollered, and rushed back in the car, rolled up the windows, locked the doors. Then I found the loudest, most obnoxious radio station I could find. I think she finally snapped during "Rock Me Amadeus," by Falco, clambered back to her feet, and started pounding on the hood as if it was the engine that had manipulated her insurance coverage instead of my father. Because I found out later that's what happened. But just then? I swear on a stack of Bibles I had no idea what the hell she was doing. She was prone to grandstanding and staging her own little street-theater dramas; the cops had been over to Tina and Dad's a half-

dozen times already, dispatched there by my mother, who'd make up some story about me being held against my will, stuffed in a closet, deprived of daylight, crapping myself, living in filth and child slavery—just your garden-variety spousal harassment. But here, hugging the hood of my T-1000 as if it had just won the Paris-to-Dakar rally, wailing like a grandmother, she had outdone herself—or *Dad* had.

You could trace this whole scene to my father's brother, Uncle Bobby. Bobby's wife, Carmen, worked for Blue Cross/Blue Shield. Paul and my mother, both employees of Kodak, had full medical coverage. Not that Bobby and Carmen were wittingly involved—most people who had the pleasure of my dad's acquaintance were unwittingly involved with him in some scheme and they had no idea, trust me. Somehow, my father had managed to claim my entire operation on my mom's insurance. Now, at first blush, what my dad pulled was unremittingly under-handed—he got the insurance company to pay without my mother's authority (yeah, big boo-hoo there) and missed a chance to take a stand ethically and be the parent who was responsible for me. But on the other hand, he did the only thing he could to provide for me, right or wrong. Yeah, yeah, you're in good hands—they just belong to someone else. But, really, I was sixteen years old. My mother wouldn't have

CHYNA

claimed me on her insurance because of her Vince Lombardi syndrome: pride and defense. And my father didn't have the money.

"You know something?" Tina said to me, a few months after the whole thing blew over. "Your dad works so hard. I'll tell you what. He's gonna make it someday." She cocked that cute little pixie hairdo of hers in Dad's direction—he was reading a book on curling (you know, those big, polished stones with the handles?), lowered the cover, and smiled that great enabling Laurer smile at me. This is the man who paid a justice of the peace ten dollars in dimes when he and my mother eloped.

"So why don't you get a regular job, Dad?" I asked him. Not in a reproving way. Fact of the matter is I adored him at that point. He could've swindled Mother Teresa, emptied the coffers of the Save the Children Foundation, and plundered the United Negro College Fund, and I would've adored him just then.

"Because, Joanie, I'd never make any real money that way." Right.

If they gave out a lifetime achievement award for scheming, Joe Laurer wouldn't just win one. He'd have it named after him. Here is a man who used the word "deal" more times in one day than a casino employee. Everything was "a business deal," "this deal," "that deal," deals everywhere. And Europe was his big, giant lollipop. Germany, Czechoslovakia, Austria, Spain (I did my senior year of high school in Madrid because Joe had fabricated some kind of foreign-exchange scholarship). We were gypsies, basically, taking advantage of whatever money exchange there was, taking advantage of the lack of technology, taking advantage of foreigners who thought they were dealing with a big-shot American deal-maker. He posed as a banker, as an economist, as a business entrepreneur. A guy who could raise cash, get it done—a visionary. While really he was pulling the wool over your eyes. He opened accounts in Switzerland with the money he saved by having us "rent" apartments in Czechoslovakia for three dollars a week—people's homes. The families of these homes didn't leave, however. They'd be there, walking around, eating, sleeping, vacuuming, while this wired, weird family slept on their couches, used their toilets, ate blood sausage at their table, and talked about Bob De Niro's new restaurant or what the Bosox were doing.

Always there was something special in it for me. "Joanie, you're so smart, they're subsidizing your senior year of high school in Madrid," and "Joanie, you're such a quick study! I know you'll learn Spanish faster than you learned to drive!" And then the deal, the backdoor scheme,

CHYNA

the part of it for him: He had me translate business documents from Spanish to English. To get the title of "Doctor" attached to your name, most people go to medical school. My father went to a noodle shop in Austria.

"Mr. Von Laurer," the shop owner greeted us.

"Doctor," my father corrected him.

5

It's Okay to Be a Little Lost

I like writers. I really do. People
who spend their lives making things up just have a special place in my heart, if you know what I'm saying. Shout-outs and mad props to our writers over at the WWF, too. It never ceases to amaze me how these guys keep coming up with different angles, different story lines, different drama. I do have a little bone to pick with them, however. I'm tempted to say that every once in a while they forget how things work in the ring, how much a move can hurt, how you fall, or where you end up when someone does a certain move on you or when you wind up draped over J.R.'s broadcasting table, waiting for your tag-team partner to power-bomb his opponent before you can get up. So, as good as they are, sometimes it seems like the writers have never been in the ring before.

After this last week, I'm even more tempted to say that they've never been in love before. I gotta tell ya, the latest story line I was involved in? Gotta be one of the hardest things I've ever done in my life. I mean, you have no idea. My boyfriend, Paul, known as Hunter, and I have been, well, experimenting with the notion of giving each other a little space. And as you probably know, his character, Triple H, is married to the character of Stephanie McMahon, Vince McMahon's daughter, who, in real life is . . . Stephanie McMahon, Vince McMahon's daughter. Well, in this latest

CHYNA

story line, Hunter and Stephanie are feuding because she's insanely jealous. And Hunter is jealous, too, because he thinks Kurt Angle has been slipping Stephanie a little Olympic gold on the sly. Anyway, according to the writers, I'm supposed to feel sorry for Hunter, give him a big hug, and tell him that I know how it feels. Duh. But I'm a professional. I'm down with it. Chyna goes with the flow, rolls with the punches. Hugs her soon-to-be-ex-boyfriend for all the world to see. Yeah, I'm cool . . . let's milk that story line for all it's worth! I mean, it's just entertainment, right?

■ ■ ■

University of Tampa, Fall 1988   God, am I a geek!!!!! My nails are short, no polish. My hair, pulled back, hidden away under my ROTC cap. No makeup. I am hating this, hating the uniforms, the field training exercises, the ungodly boring courses in military history.

"But, Muffin—having ROTC on your résumé is huge. It'll help you later. Trust me," Colonel Von Laurer reminded me. You have to remember that the man who could sell condoms by the case to a choir of castrati was still my great hero, although lately I was beginning to see a few chinks in his (fake) armor. Like getting me into the University of Tampa.

"Honey, it's all taken care of," he told me, but when I went to register, they held me up—in front of all these other students in line. More humiliation for Joanie, who hated losers.

CHYNA

"Will you save my spot?" I asked this big dude in line. I mention this guy because I would meet him again, only we wouldn't be standing, if you catch my drift. I found a phone, called my father.

"What's going on, Pop? Everybody's getting through registration but me."

"Now, now, Muffin, it's probably just a little mix-up. Give me ten minutes."

I'm back in line with the big dude, who's checking me out when this administrative assistant comes up to me, smiles.

"Miss Laurer? You're okay. Your registration's completed."

So I took ROTC because it would look good on my résumé. Follow the plan, Joanie. And being phobic about losers, I went into it whole hog. I shot M-16s. I rappelled off giant towers. We dug foxholes. We crawled on our bellies through slop and mud. We went on recons in the middle of the night with a map. We followed clues to where something like a box of ammo or whatever was buried.

"LAURER! GIVE ME TWENTY PULLS!!" Captain Cook would holler, a fat, ecstatic smile across his face. Not because he was mean, but because I could do them and half the corps couldn't. I was his good example. I won plaques and awards named after dead generals.

It's Okay to Be a Little Lost

"Oh, Joanie, I'm so proud of you," my father gushed. He was an oil well of compliments (which is to say, he was greasing me good). "I knew you could do it, you're so smart. You hold your head up high; you, Muffin, are head and shoulders above everybody else." Yadda yadda yadda.

Funny thing, hindsight. If I ran into me at that school now? Boy, what a tight-ass! What a tool! What a Goody Two-shoes! Miss On-Time. Research paper? Done. Done weeks before it was due because I was a spaz about meeting deadlines, about not failing. I didn't drink, I didn't socialize. I was everybody's good example. And that meant one thing. I was ripe for the pickin'.

They made me an RA. It's a kind of dorm supervisor. You made sure everyone obeyed the rules. No drinking, no parties. In other words, no fun. They made me a Homecoming candidate. Not the students—they would never vote for me. But the teachers could nominate someone, and Joanie Laurer was every instructor's dream.

So what's the deal with these slackers? Skipping courses, going out to lie around the pool during lunch, getting off. How do they do that? Don't they care? I was curious and dying to find out about them. I wanted to shake my finger at them and say, "Shame, shame, everybody knows your name!" You want the truth? I was vacuum-packed. I was repressed. How bad? I took summer courses. I stayed

CHYNA

at the dorm as the RA. Enter Joanie the benevolent: Kids in the dorm had parties. They drank, left their doors open. I knew about it but decided to relax the rules a little. The drinking age was twenty-one and they were all doing it legally, responsibly. One night there was a party on the second floor. They were playing "She Drives Me Crazy," that Fine Young Cannibals song that gets into your head like a virus. I'd rather get bikini-waxed with molten lead than have to listen to that song. I hated it. So I went down there with the intention of Frisbee-ing the CD into the stratosphere.

"Hey, you want a drink?" somebody asked me. Of course, I refused until they put it in the form of a game. "Oh, come on, loosen up. We're playing quarters."

It's a drinking game. You bounce a quarter toward a glass. If the quarter falls in the glass, you get to pick anyone around the circle to take a shot. If you want to see the RA get drunk off her ass, you keep picking Joanie. An hour later:

"Yeah, yeah, my, my father helped get the Shah of Iran out. Yeah, that was after he fooled the mayor of Dublin into believing he was an astronaut," I was babbling. Next thing I know someone's unbuttoning my top. There was a gap of time that is so lost it could've started some relativity-continuum nightmare. But when I woke up there was a dick in my mouth while another guy was drilling for oil at the other end. The two

CHINA
It's Okay to Be a Little Lost

guys were football players—one of them was the guy at registration. Did I consent? Not on your life. So much for quarters. Anyway, now I can't stand the sight of parking meters.

A short time later, I heard from my father.

"Muffin, you need to join the Peace Corps. It'll be great
for your—" Résumé. Right.

■ ■ ■

You see the pattern yet? Uniforms. Regimentation. Soldier.
Follower. Sheep. That was young Joanie, under the spell
of . . . of what? My father? Yeah, maybe a little. But he was
just the delivery system. I wanted to be wanted, I wanted to
be cared for, I wanted respect. And it took me a while to realize that I wasn't going to get any respect until I learned to
take care of myself. College, ROTC, graduation, the Peace
Corps—these were all just words, really, somebody else's
plan. I graduated from college and skipped the ceremonies
to save the cap-and-gown money. Did the old man's bid-
ding—went into the Peace Corps, slept on a dirt floor in
some Guatemalan hut for two months without electricity
until I just plain couldn't hack it anymore. You know what? I
didn't have the balls for the Peace Corps. The Peace Corps, a
wonderful humanitarian organization, doesn't build character (especially if you're doing it for "your résumé, Muffin"), it
requires it. And at the time, I was a lightweight. I came
home; my dad was probably madder than I'd ever seen him

CHYNA

before, at least sober. I was big, physically fit, powerful, and weak. So I drifted. And there's no better place to find yourself than in the Florida Keys. Look at it on the map. It's the place where the Continental United States starts to unravel, it's another fucking world . . .

His name was . . . well, let's just call him Tom, which isn't his real name. Big dude, probably six-foot-two if you got him in a lineup—which happened often. Tom served time, about five years in federal prison for drug smuggling. He was what you would call a mule—brought the drugs in from Colombia by boat, in his boot, up his ass, whatever. You do that in the Keys, you gotta be a little whacked to begin with because everyone was crooked, and everyone was involved. Dirty FBI agents, double-crossing money-men, snitches, rip-offs. The only people who made money were the suppliers and the lawyers. I admit that it was crazy to be with a man like Tom, but the fact was he had balls, and he was a badass motherfucker. Frankly, I found that exciting. He had enormous courage—a trait I lacked back then—even if it was somewhat misdirected. I thrived on that.

I was working at a place called Mellon's. Is it possible that a franchise like Hooters could be copied? Only in Key West. Tom and I became involved romantically. Translation: I worked, he drank. I came home, we fought. When we

CHINA

It's Okay to Be a Little Lost

weren't fighting, he'd talk about whose throat he was going to slice next. Hopefully not mine!

Tom had a dog, a pit bull named Shitter because he crapped on anything of value—the couch, your clothes, the carpet, etc. He crapped because Tom literally scared the shit out of him. He beat the poor animal senseless. I did what I could to save Shitter from Tom's half-coherent wrath by cleaning up after the dog, loving him into a sort of resigned canine Zen place, where the beatings started to not scare him as much. When Tom realized Shitter would no longer cower or back off, he stopped beating him. That's when he started on me. You're probably thinking about how pathetic this situation sounds—to be involved with the very type of loser, lowlife pond scum that I always hated. And it was. I'd like to think we were codependent—after all, was it really any different from what I'd been used to domestically? And it would be easier to swallow if I could say I felt sorry for him. You could even say I owed it to him—literally. I had shitty,

CHYNA

low-paying jobs, no health insurance, and the cysts were back. Tom paid for the operation. But more than anything, I needed to see the darkest side of life, to go under, to see the demon and go, BOO! All I can say is don't try this at home.

I came home one night from an aerobics class. That was my one release, my one guilty pleasure, I guess. I tried to take care of my body. It was hot, the windows were open, and as I got out of my car, I could hear this murmuring drifting out of the house, from the living room windows. I looked in and Tom was talking to Shitter.

"Now, Shitter—don't be upset. I gotta do what I gotta do and that's all," he told the dog through gulps of whiskey. "She's doing this to herself." The "she" he was referring to, of course, was me.

"Where you been." Tom looked at the floor when he said this, and said it without asking, as if there was no right answer. Before I could even try to respond, he threw me across the room. I was gonna have a bruise the size of a place mat on my back. I stood up. He lingered, reared a little, the way a python does before it darts at you with its fangs. Then I screamed in his face: "That's gonna scare me, you fuck!!!!? HUH? You wanna kill me??? You wanna make me cry, you wanna hurt me, big man!!!? COME ON!!!! COME ON!!!!!" Well, he just stood there. I think Tom knew there was no middle ground for him. Like Shitter. He went the limit, he

CHYNA

was immune to the violence. I think Tom knew he was either going to kill me or leave me alone. I never saw him again.

I moved in with my friend Suzy for a while, then got a small place of my own. More odd jobs. Sang in a band that never got paid, served cocktails to car salesmen in some bar until it burned down, talked to freaks on a 900 line until I thought I'd heard every possible way to have sex without having sex. Then I saw the ad for flight-attendant school and it seemed like a godsend (although, what was it with me and uniforms?). The ghostrider put me in the hospital and the friendly skies flew away without me. Suzy later told me that she heard Shitter died of heartworms.

"Why don't you come up and live with me," my sister, Kathy, offered. "There's nothing to prove down there anymore, Joan."

CHINA

It's Okay to Be a Little Lost

6

Never Underestimate the Value of a Good Education

Let's review: ROTC was a burn.

The University of Tampa kind of, ahem, sucked. Studying to join the FBI and Secret Service was just another version of Where's Waldo on a ten-most-wanted list, and although flight-attendant school taught me how to smile at will and the proper way to fill a coffee cup at twenty-nine thousand feet (*never*, I repeat, NEVER extend over a passenger's lap to pour), I crashed and burned before takeoff. Kathy got me an entry-level job at MobileCom selling beepers. My face healed. Other parts of me were gonna take a little longer . . .

Now, the beeper-selling job was golden, and shout-outs to Kathy for landing me the job. Having cash in the bank and money in my pockets was a novel experience and something I was really beginning to like, the screams I'd hear coming from the alleys of the drug-dealing crack hoods where I did most of my business notwithstanding. Incidentally, I sold three beepers in one day to a really nice Jamaican fella. He paid cash, which is always a plus, but in order to get it out of his pocket he had to set the Mercedes car fender he was carrying on the sidewalk.

I continued my workouts—which also helped prepare me for an occasional altercation with that not-so-rare beeper customer who got it in his head that if he bought one, he should get one free. Forget about the difference between men and women—the hard reality of muscles

CHYNA

makes even the cockiest little rip-off artist lose just a little of that hard-on for thievery. Anyway, the money was great. I was making close to sixty grand a year, bought a new car, and was living the single life with moderate success. So the idea of going back to school seemed a little counterproductive, a little unrealistic, and, yeah, maybe a little foolish . . .

"You dumb shit!" Kathy smacks me in the arm when I mention Killer Kowalski's school again. "'Kowalski, Kowalski, Kowalski,' over and over. You know, I seriously think you might have brain damage." I could barely hear her over the music. We had taken up belly dancing. Bachelor parties, weddings, bar mitzvahs, that sort of thing. And we were accredited. We had belly-dancing diplomas from Zebeida's Harem. Zebeida was this grandmother who ran a belly-dancing school out of Tewkesbury, Massachusetts. Ten bucks a lesson, Tuesday nights. For an old lady, Zebeida—her real name is Helen Perry, mistress of the singing bellygram—knew how to shake it, to be sure, but her real talent was in understanding the male animal (we'd talk for hours about them) and costume making. This woman was Michelangelo with a bead stringer. And sequins? Forget about it. This lady flat-out knew sequins and how to use them as a weapon of enticement.

Tonight we're working a fight party; Mike Tyson, boxing for the first time since he's been released from prison, is on Pay-Per-View. Kathy and I are wearing matching platinum

Never Underestimate the Value of a Good Education

wigs, black halter tops, Victoria's Secret boxing shorts. "Listen to me—you have a little self-respect now, some security, self-confidence, and you want to go half-cocked looking for this Kowalski guy?" She wasn't really mad, just being sisterly. And frankly, she was right. I can't even remember who told me about Killer Kowalski in the first place, and for that matter, he could be retired or dead for all I knew. A guy walked by with his big mouth open as wide as the laws of physics will allow, then stuck his tongue at us. Nice.

"You gotta quit this Kowalski business. You're probably gonna wind up losing your job, you know," she says, giving the guy the finger, "and honestly, I don't even think it's the wrestling any-more. I just think you're obsessed, you're on one of your tunnel-vision missions." Maybe she had a point. But ever since we saw it on TV—she and I together, laughing our asses off at the guys in their costumes, tossing each other around, growl-ing, vamping—I was hooked. The girl wrestlers? Forget it. They were all T&A and not nearly as interesting. Wrestling. "I can do that!" I remem-ber shouting at the TV.

CHYNA

Never Underestimate the Value of a Good Education

"Sure, sure, we'll do it together. Tag team." Kathy laughed into her Chianti, but there it was in all its epic ambition, its winking boorishness, its harmless heroics. "I CAN DO THAT!" I got up, paced, pointed at the set. "LOOK! Look at those guys! Look at their faces! They're having—"

"What? What're they having?"

"Fun." And I wanted in. It was kooky, it was wrong-headed, it was MY CHOICE. And I didn't know the first thing about it. Was there a how-to book I could read? That's what Laurer the Lout would've done, anyway. Read up. Bluffed. Not me. I wanted from the ground floor up. I wasn't gonna fake my way into this. I wanted to know everything about it. Somebody mentioned a school.

I spent two nights scouring the yellow pages for gyms and wrestling schools. Some geezer told me Kowalski lived in the Salem, Massachusetts, area, but damned if I could find his school.

"Hey, Big Momma! Show us some titty!!!" Some drunk with his necktie wrapped around his forehead is yelling at me. Maybe I should look harder . . .

Long before Mike Tyson had a hankering for earlobes, there was Wladek Kowalski — six and a half feet tall, built like a caveman's club, and stronger than dirt. There was this match in Montreal (Kowalski was from Windsor, Canada) back in 1952. He was wrestling Canadian legend Yukon Eric

CHYNA

and inadvertently ripped off a part of Yukon's ear in the middle of a knee drop—and this was after he was known as "Killer." There were other wrestling schools, sure, but Kowalski was the shit, the man, the professor—that's the, er, earplay I was picking up, anyway. Prince Albert, Triple H, and Perry Saturn all trained under Killer. You want to act, you go to Strasberg. You want to dance, you go to the Joffrey. You want to wrestle? You find Kowalski. So I thought, anyway.

Sometime around eleven, after the Tyson fight (it ended early—first-round KO), I was determined to call every Kowalski in the phone book. And not because I don't enjoy belly dancing, mind you. But Kathy was right, even if she was half-naked and wearing a ho' wig when she expressed her opinion. I had a thing about challenges. I got off on long odds, and just now Kowalski, in all his Polish Speedo splendor, was my Holy Grail. I got out the phone book—the residential one, this time. I mean, how many Wladek (Walter, if you're New World) Kowalskis can there be? One. In Malden, Massachusetts. I punch out the number. Someone picks up after three rings. When the guy says hello, it sounds like I've called Kraków or something. Sounds like he's got a mouthful of sausage and no teeth, like he's about to fall asleep or just woke up from an episode of *The Twilight Zone:*

"Halloah?"

"Um, hi, I know it's late, but is this Walter Kowalski?"

"Yah. And it's also late, is what it is."

"Like . . . is this Killer?"

"Yah, yah, yah, Killer, yah—what the hell you want?"

"You have a wrestling school—"

"No. Not school. *Insteetoote.*"

"What?"

"Insteetoote. Not school."

"Oh, *institute*—"

"Killer Kowalski Insteetoote of Professional Wrestling. I filed taxes already—good-bye."

"No, wait, wait. I want to learn to wrestle." I caught him before he hung up. There was a long pause, and I could hear him breathing. Then he slid his hand over the mouthpiece so I couldn't hear and he hollered at someone, then silence again—except for the heavy, nasal breathing, as if an ox was sitting on his chest.

"Uh, hello?" I tried again.

"Two thousand dollars."

"Excuse me?"

"You want to learn to wrestle? Two thousand dollars. No checks." Most of the time you couldn't make out what he was trying to say. Unless the subject was money. Then he came through loud and clear.

I am up at the crack of dawn the next day—actually, I never went to sleep—and in the car, making the forty-five-

Never Underestimate the Value of a Good Education

minute drive to Malden with visions of stardom dancing in my head. I am going to wrestle! I mean, *wrestle*—not follow some male tushe around and be his trinket. I am going to bury the women! I tell you what? The men, goddamn it! I want the boys! Bring on the beards, the three-legged monsters with the trouser mouse roaring in their tights, because I want them! But first things first.

There's a better than even chance that the Killer Kowalski Institute of Professional Wrestling doesn't do a whole lot of walk-in business. The place is on a one-way street on the second floor of some empty old warehouse. You go around the back, up some rickety mob-hit-type stairs. I walk in and boom! Suddenly I'm in a bad, low-budget kung fu movie. Guys doing karate in the I-just-burned-my-hand style. Big, overweight bouncer-type guys awkwardly throwing each other around the way you'd wrestle with your mattress at home if you had to move it by yourself. The place is furnished with yard-sale rejects—unmatching chairs, cast-iron weights painted that awful green, a bathroom you wouldn't use if you were wearing a thousand-dollar evening gown and had the runs. There's a converted boxing ring in the middle of the room with two pairs of human legs extending out from under it and hammering sounds coming from beneath. Either the plumbing ran under the ring and these guys were working on it or

CHYNA

they were actually working on the underside of the ring. Whatever. (It turned out to be the latter; Walter's ring was constantly collapsing, with the two-by-fours holding up the canvas constantly snapping. When I was there, the two guys were replacing the wood with steel beams—which would hurt like hell to fall against, but I digress.)

Just outside of the ring, an old man, mid-seventies, wearing a gray hairpiece that's so cheap you can see the rubber curling up at the nape of his neck, is shouting into the face of this poor, reed-thin twenty-something kid with really bad skin. To drive his point home, the old man whacks the kid over the head with a phone book—Walter Kowalski, demonstrating his people skills. When I step in, Walter turns around, looks at me, then turns back to the ring. Two guys are reversing each other over and over until one of them throws the other over his head. The guy lands flat on his back and there is this muffled groan from the two guys working under the ring. Walter grunts something that is taken as a compliment by the two guys in the ring. Finally, he ambles over to me, moving like a giant shrimp walking on its hind legs. I tell him I'm the one who spoke with him on the phone, and before I can finish my sentence, he's got his hand out for the money. Since at first blush I am not terribly impressed with, well, let's start with the decor, I tell Walter that I just want to watch for a while.

CHYNA

"Waatch? Huh. Fleeex yaw ahm."

"Excuse me?" Those first few days, I couldn't under-stand a word he was saying. His Polish accent was so thick. It wasn't pidgin English, it was a goddamn turkey. "Gawn. Fleeex yah ahm!" I finally figure out he wants me to flex my arm, because somebody is pantomiming it for me.

I make a muscle and he squeezes it, hides his reaction, but I can tell he's a little impressed. "How mooch do you leeeft?" He's walking me over to the weights. Some of the other guys are bench-pressing about 180 pounds. I stop at 235—not because I can't lift any heavier (I've done 315 on a good day, plenty of rest) but I figure showing up some of these guys just wouldn't be the best way to start things off. But again, I can see Walter's impressed—his wig keeps shifting with his eyebrows. Then, I'm guessing for my ben-efit, because I still haven't given him any money, he claps his hands and has everyone gather around because he has something to say. But before he can begin we all have to pull the two guys in the ring apart—they've wrestled each other into some kind of ridiculous draw where they have each other by the head. One of them is wearing this black T-shirt that says BEBE in silver sequins. The other one has really bad gas and farts every time he applies pressure to Bebe. The guy braces his thighs—*bloweee!*

"You tapping out, you fuck??!!? You tapping out!!?" The

CHYNA

guy in the Bebe T-shirt keeps hollering ("tapping out" means you're surrendering because the hold your opponent has you in is too painful, i.e., Chris Benoit's cross-face Crippler hold) until he realizes it's Walter trying to break them up. But Bebe and the guy with the bad gas are *shooting* now—a shoot being a real fight—and Walter couldn't break up a smoke ring, so the rest of us have to pull them apart.

"All right, all right, everyone." Walter claps his bony, misshapen hands again. "This is what you all need to remember: The whole thing about wrestling is what you think. When you think, you become. Okay? Thinking, becoming. Think big and shoot for the moon. Be good to your guts. Eat what grows from the ground. Never demean yourself." The guy with the gas cuts a fart that nearly blows out a back wall, but Walter just acts like he hasn't heard it— and, for that matter, the other guys are ignoring it, too. That's when I realize what a really nasty guy Walter is. He's nasty and compassionate and accepting and dismissing all at once. And I love him for it. "Look at yourself as being world champion and you will become one. Drink water with cayenne pepper. That's rule number two. Third rule is you obey rules one and two. Okay—you, little big lady"— he's motioning with his fingers for me to step forward—"do you know what a body slam is?" Before I can answer, Walter cuts the guy in the Bebe T-shirt from the herd, has Bebe

Never Underestimate the Value of a Good Education

standing in front of me. "See if you can pick him up. One arm over the shoulder, the other in the crotch, there, okay, easy, easy then—" BLAM! I slammed Bebe down. He's lying there, glaring up at me, and Walter is laughing, then everyone's laughing, even Bebe starts to laugh—until he leg-whips me. "That's gonna bruise," I'm thinking, "that's really gonna show up in the fitness contest next week"— and before I can blink, I'm flat on my back. Bebe throws all his weight on my chest, which is okay, but when he snatches up one of my knees, I kind of take offense—it just seems oddly, well . . . sexual—and I impulsively throw him off my body. I'm laughing nervously because I don't want Bebe to think I thought it was sexual or anything, because I want them all to know I can take it as well as dish it out— but nobody is smiling, I mean, NOBODY. They're all gawking at me like I just bent a whole place setting's worth of silverware by twitching my nose.

"Jesus H. Christ, she's strong," this guy finally mutters.

Walter's got one hand on his hip, the other tugging on a big, hairy ear. Jerks his head at me like he wants me to step forward, the sudden jerk making his hairpiece shift to one side. For a second, he looks like a guy in a sixties rock band who's time-traveled and aged a hundred years except for his hair.

"You got a plaine?" he asks me.

CHYNA

"A plane?" Was he serious?

"Not plane. Plaaine. Plaaine!"

"*Plan*. Do I have a plan? Is that what you're asking?"

"What's your plaine?"

This was about as good a question as I have ever been asked—and remember, the FBI interviewed me. Since, at the time, I had no idea how scheming and cutthroat Walter could be—this is a guy who prides himself on loyalty but uses it to keep you down, to keep you from going out on your own; this is the guy whose pat answer whenever recruiters from the WCW or WWF would show up was "He's not ready!!"— I gave him a very straight and open answer: Simple. I wanted to become a professional wrestler.

"Uh-huh. Who you gonna wrestle?" he asked, which at the time seemed like the *worst* question I had ever been asked—and remember, the FBI interviewed me. I mean, *duh*. I was gonna wrestle other women wrestlers.

"Silly," he said.

"Silly? Women have been wrestling longer than the men. That's silly?"

"You're too big, too strong. Gonna be silly," he said, walking away. Then added, "You coming tomorrow?"

"To watch, yeah . . ." I said. I wasn't quite ready to commit my money to a crazy man with a ring that had legs coming out of it. And I might have to pop for a translator.

Never Underestimate the Value of a Good Education

"Fine. Gonna cost you two thousand dollars to watch."

I came back a week later, paid him the cash. Not so much because I had time to think it over, but because it seemed, well, predestined, out of my hands, a road without a fork, straight, straight, straight—part of a master *plaine*.

Me and phones. For a while, I couldn't get away from them—phones, beepers, belly dancing—it's all the same. You're using an instrument to get a message across. When I was in Florida, as I said, I worked for a 900 number for a while. I know what you're thinking—forget about it. It wasn't phone sex (for me, anyway). It was a chat line. We got paid for the length of time people stayed on the line, complained about school, bellyached about their jobs, girlfriends, parents, neighborhoods, and so on. You got paid by this quota system, a percentage of the time they spent on the line, so, of course, you do what you can to keep them blabbering away. I really hated it because you'd get these cheerful little perverts—"What're you wearing?" If you don't respond, you're just screwing yourself out of minutes. You start to tell them and pretty soon you hear the heavy breathing and it all turns to crap anyway. I had one guy—called every freakin' night. Foot fetish. How did I know? "Um, hi, it's me again. Say, I'm on my feet all day with my job and I was wondering. How would you treat a corn on your big toe? Really? What about one

CHYNA

on your middle toe? Huh. Ever had a heel blister? Gee. You know what's even worse? A callous right on the ball of your left foot—you know, that soft, fleshy part that can almost work like a hand if you want it to?" That's how I knew.

And belly dancing? Everyone knows what the message is there, but what the hell. Then beepers and pagers. This was my big-money mother lode, as I mentioned earlier. Likewise, it was Kathy who warned me, during the belly dancing–Mike Tyson party, that wrestling would cost me my job. She was right.

I paid Walter his money, then came to the school as much as I could. After a few months of fitting wrestling school, bodybuilding, and my job at MobilCom into my *plaine,* something had to give. And it was about to.

■ ■ ■

"NO. The boy will be *keeeled,*" Walter would rampage into the phone, making sure all of us heard. "He's not ready!" The boy will be killed and he's not ready. We heard this whenever the WWF or the WCW or the ECW called or showed up, interested in new talent. Walter was very possessive about all of us back then. Nice to be wanted, huh? Truth was Walter just kept you down—as long as you allowed it. He taught us a few of the basics—I did so many clothesline drills my arms were black and blue for a year and a half. But most of the time Walter sat in a chair and

CHYNA

watched these poor, hopeless eighteen-year-old high school dropouts climb up to the top ropes and jump off, pretend to be The Rock, or tear each other's clothes to shreds until Walter eventually fell asleep. "You! You're not ready! You'll end up keeeled! Don't look at me like that, little asshole! I'll keel you myself!" But he had a roof, a ring, a few warm bodies to try things on, and he did have connections. Which was a hell of a lot more than I had, so I stuck it out at the insteetoote.

After some time, I developed a pretty effective routine. Most of the day I spent watching, observing, learning what not to do. When the ring thinned out, I did most of my practicing with this guy I developed a car-pool relationship with. Freight Train Dan and I alternated driving in together, and Freight Train, a really good guy, actually knew some good moves and routines.

We're working out one afternoon; no heat. I mean the gym, not Dan. Walter kept the place cold because heat cost money. Dan was showing me how to bounce off the ropes and into your opponent's body. Our heads accidentally collided and *kapow,* I go down, stunned.

"Joanie, Joanie!" Dan's yelling. At least I think he is, because I can see his lips moving, but I can't hear him, I'm so stunned. "Walter! Get some ice! Joanie! Joanie, how many fingers? Can you see my fingers?" I can hear Dan now: "Walter!

Never Underestimate the Value of a Good Education

Get some ice!" There's a crowd of pimple-faced wanna-be wrestlers gathered around me now, looking gravely down at me, as if I'd lost all my front teeth or my nose was missing. And if I needed ice, all I had to do was use my hands. The fucker just wouldn't budge on the heat.

"Gnarly," one of the student-savants mutters, and backs away. Dan helps me to my feet, Walter comes with the ice, shoves it at me, then notices my face and shudders in fear.

"You signed *weever*. Remember? You signed *weever*—"

I stagger over to the mirror above the sink, look between the cracks and the AC/DC sticker, peer into it, and am startled by what I see. Walter is at my heels like a terrier, blocking my view of myself, but I push him away. Because I have this glorious shiner, my first real black eye. It was . . . beautiful.

"You signed *weever*—"

"Yeah, yeah, yeah, Walter, I signed the fucking waiver, I'm not gonna sue you. Somebody get me a camera. Dan, Dan—take my picture! Take my picture!"

Freight Train Dan and I encouraged each other. Well, actually, we were married. Or at least it seemed like that because I really henpecked the poor guy. Nice guy, really nice guy, like Jerry. It's such a drag. Time marches on, but the nice guys just always seem to take baby steps. Dan was hoping to be discovered.

"You gotta get out there and make it happen for yourself, Dan," I would chide him. "Take some pictures of yourself, set up a fucking camera in your spare time, get some stuff over to the WWF."

"Oh, well, Walter's gonna do all that when he thinks I'm ready."

"Walter's never gonna do that for you, Dan. Don't you get it? He's a nasty old man who wants you to stay right here and do shows for less than nothing."

"But I feel loyal to Walter."

"Well, you can feel loyal to Walter all you want, but he's not gonna get you into the WWF. Only you can do that."

"What about you? You're still here," Dan, a little out of character, told me one day. Good point.

Never Underestimate the Value of a Good Education

7

*Wrestling
Is Fake*

We are crossing the border from

Canada into the state of Washington. Me and Terry, my usual travel partner, got the rented Monte Carlo with GPS this time so we'll be able to find that great little Italian restaurant near the Space Needle. The line through the checkpoint is moving slowly, and now coming to a complete stop—three guys in their mid-twenties are putting up a fight with the Canadian border guards. They're either drunk, stoned, or smuggling drugs back into the United States, and the poor border guys (who would actually make really good fake security guards for the WWF) can't get the cuffs on them. While the line is held up, I climb out to stretch my legs. Terry stays in the car, enters the street address for this totally golden Italian restaurant in Seattle we want to eat at. At the rate we're going—which is not at all—we'll never make it before the place closes. And without a good meal, I'm gonna need a shovel to the temple to get to sleep.

Sleep? Yeah, in your dreams—which you're not gonna have because you can't get to sleep. You're on the road two hundred days a year crossing four time zones, getting in late, getting up early, driving to a location, wired from the road, wired from the performance—your body's spent! Sleep and how to get it becomes a real problem. You have choices: sleep therapy—which I tried and failed—or some

CHYNA

kind of homeopathic way. Melatonin, kava root, berry root, warm milk. What do you do late at night when you can't sleep? I've written down half of the 800 numbers I've seen on late-night TV for cheese, greatest hits of the eighties, butt-busters, dolls, face cream, knives, you name it . . . I get up in the morning, see these numbers, and wonder, "What was I thinking?" If I don't take Grandpa's Cough Syrup, I'm up until four or five in the morning. Every night, different hotel, different pillows—it's bloody fucking murder. Maybe your body's sore, you're stressed, you're living out of a suitcase. Tonight, we'll be lucky if we get three hours of rest.

Watching the checkpoint commotion, I hear the door slam in the car behind us. Out of the corner of my eye I can see this big guy with a swollen gut lumber aggressively toward our car. A real big-ass clown. Sleeveless Metallica T-shirt, with the Kentucky Waterfall haircut and a piece of swing-set chain attached to his wallet. *Trouble*.

"We've been made," I warn Terry. Code for "We've been recognized."

"How bad?"

"Dresses left—big time." Terry motions for me to get back in, but before I can the big guy's all over me, a strong vibe of tainted, spoiled masculinity making his whole body move in a blubbery jitter. He was one. One of these people who listens way too much to that warped inner voice, the

CHYNA *Wrestling Is Fake*

one that tells him (or her, I've seen both) that the world is not nearly as complicated as everyone says and all you need to navigate it is a pair of balls and a little nerve. The end result is usually gunfire, rape, regret—a mess. This particular guy says nothing, just keeps coming. I'm bracing to pop him one if he puts his hands on me—there are crazy people out there, believe me, and they'll try anything.

And Walter—remember Walter? Well, I do, especially in potentially dangerous situations. Walter is like my Obi-Wan Kenobi: "Remember the force, Joanie." Because most of what Walter taught us was bad. He never taught us anything about the psychology of pro wrestling, or how to physically tell a story in the ring. The ebb and flow, the heroism in taking a punch, coming back from the dead. Hell, you can learn more playing Mortal Kombat. You see the little animated figures just after their lungs have been ripped out, how they teeter, stagger, fall dead. You could learn more watching a bad B-western or a Bruce Lee movie. You can pick up more about storytelling and psychology spending ten minutes with Vince McMahon than spending two grand on Walter and his vegetarian sermons. Vince taught me about adrenaline and how it changes your perception of time. You're pumped up, going a million miles an hour, catapulting yourself off the ropes at your opponent, body-smashing him into the ring. You're SO ready to grab

CHYNA

him, with so much adrenaline coursing through your body that it affects your hearing. With your pulse beating that fast, the eustachian tubes get temporarily blocked. And if you can't hear, then you can't hear the crowd. You can't hear them reacting, feeding off of your energy. "If you can't hear, you take a beat," Vince told me. "You let the audience come up, come up, come up." Walter never taught us anything like that, and even if he'd tried, we'd never been able to understand him. What Walter did best was teach us how to street-fight or "shoot" fight. Arm bars, choke holds, and sleeper holds that, if you performed properly, would cut your enemies' breathing off so they'd pass out. "Night-night," Walter would grin, resting his craggy face on his hands, with that fake, limp hair shifting on his scalp like a glacier of soggy shredded wheat. Walter turned us into lethal weapons, showed us fulcrum moves where you manipulate a person's joints to make him move with you. Walter taught us the real stuff—stuff you NEVER use on the mat and hope to God you never need to use off it. But this stooge is bearing down on me in all of his fat-headed eminence, and I have to remind myself to just be cool, to not believe my own bullshit.

"Hey, Chyna! You think you can take me?" The Big Ass glares—I smell Molson—then breaks into a shit-eating grin. "Just kidding, just kidding. You rock, Chyna, you totally

Wrestling Is Fake

rock. I was there when you lost to Chris Jericho—you got robbed, that sucked," and blah, blah, blah. This guy, as it turns out, is just lonely. Wants to talk a little wrestling, go back to his pals and tell them how he called me out, and that's cool. Roll with the punches. On the road, you protect yourself by being careful. And there it is: Pro wrestling, a great big jubilee of confrontation, taught me how to be less confrontational. If there's one way I've changed the most over the years, I think it's being able to withdraw when my inclination is to engage, to not be such a lackey to my impulses. Don't get me wrong, though. Being mad as hell and not taking it anymore has its place . . .

■ ■ ■

"Jesus, Walter! Will you turn the fucking heat on?" Kowalski just ignored me, sat in that stupid deck chair of his, and watched these two kids who had to still be in their teens try and climb up to the top rope without falling. They were working out some kind of suplex of the ropes—or they would have been if they could make it to the top, but they kept stumbling, getting ankle-tangled in the ropes. "Walter!" I wasn't gonna let him off this time. "Turn the damn heat on! If you're not gonna get up, at least tell me where the thermostat is and I'll do it."

"You don't need heat. Heat makes you weak." Walter's on his feet now, stalking toward me in his hard shoes. His

sweatpants, always bagged out in the knees, looked like they might've seen the '36 Olympics. "Heat makes you lazy. You want to be lazy? Go somewhere else. Go eat a steak. Go have your Salisbury steak. Heeeet. When I wrestled, we wrestled outside in blizzards without gloves or heat. I let my hands freeze hard as ice blocks and hit the guy with them. *You*. *You*"—Walter's pointing at this ex–subway conductor and to the guy who just left his gay partner because he wanted to be straight—"clothesline drill with crabby, here."

"No, Walter, NO MORE CLOTHESLINES. THAT'S IT. NO MORE."

"She's crabby," he says, referring to me in the third person. Usually, that meant he was ready to blow. "No? Don't want school? Don't want to learn? You want heat? EVERY-BODY GO HOME!! YOU'RE ALL A BUNCH OF FUCK-ING IDIOTS!!!"

"No, Walter. I'M NOT LEAVING."

"See this? Never say yes to women. I bring in women and women are only trouble. They refuse to train, they refuse to leave. Uh-huh. You want a refund, you forget it. I taught you more than three thousand dollars' worth of wrestling."

"It was two thousand, Walter."

"Two? No, no, it was three. Definitely three," he insists, conspicuously avoiding eye contact with the students who probably paid three thousand. "I CAN'T TAKE THIS. EVERYBODY OUT! You especially!"

"I lost my job today and this is all I have! I'm not leaving!"

It was true. Sort of. I had lost my job at MobilCom a couple of days before. Laid off. No more pocket full o' cash. No more health insurance, and most of all, no more making a change on someone else's terms. At least that's what it felt like at the time—that I'd failed at something and it was time to go (slink) away. I'd miss the steady routine, kind of like that Matt Dillon line in *Drugstore Cowboy* about how a junkie knows exactly what to expect, how to feel because it's right there on the pill bottle. And MobilCom was a big fix. I had my own territory over northeastern Massachusetts, including Lowell, Andover, and Marlboro. Some areas, like Lawrence, were Puerto Rican. Which was right in my wheelhouse, since thanks to Jose de Laurer, I spoke fluent Spanish. And I networked. One of my, er, business associates was Pedro, who had a legit green card (in someone else's name) and wore a hair net. The silver crucifix hanging around his neck had to be the size of a cruise-ship anchor. I remember the drug dealers who used to roam around South Miami. They would use pit bulls to intimidate, and they always had one or two on a leash to create fear. Pedro had a pet ferret, really a very gentle animal, but the enemies of Pedro *"piensan que Pedro es un animal."* With the ferret on a leash everyone thought he was loco and left

CHYNA

him pretty much alone. By the way, Pedro often called me "Mamacita"—funny coincidence, right?

So I'd give Pedro a bag full of beepers, maybe fifty in total. He'd sell 'em at the list price and we'd go 60–40 on the profit (Pedro and the ferret took the 40 percent). I had the same arrangement with maybe a half-dozen other *eses,* but Pedro was always my favorite. One day I went to meet Pedro. He was sobbing uncontrollably. He had the ferret palmed in one hand. Some of Pedro's friends told me that a Dalmatian had attacked the ferret.

And, boy, talk about carpetbagger capitalism. I had this quota—sell X number of contracts a month. I'd be in these neighborhoods where the currency was food stamps and welfare checks, but folks kept shelling out cash for beepers and then signed up for service—six-month minimum. Most of them would end up unable to pay their monthly bill, but I still got mine, quota-wise. My bosses never knew how I did business, all they knew was that Joanie Laurer knew how to get it done, didn't she? "We want you to think about staying with us for a long time, Joanie." "What's your secret, Joanie?" "Joanie could sell beepers to the Amish." I think I did, once—a *lapsed* Amish. Once a week we had a sales meeting. I'd put on makeup, dress up in my suit, come on with the supersize earnestness, then go home and change back into my sneakers and sweatsuit so I'd look like everybody else

CHYNA Wrestling Is Fake

when I went back into the hood to hustle. I guess even then I was living a dual life.

From the time I started at Walter's school, my beeper quota went steadily south. The suits called me in and gave me a straight-faced story about how the company was in the middle of a merger, meaning they'd be downsizing, and people would be losing their jobs. It was all meant to light a fire under my ass, but I knew what I wanted the minute I got my first black eye—I wanted to wrestle. Next time they called me in I got the pink slip. "You haven't met your quota in three months," my boss said, frowning, and I was gone. Pedro's ferret was dead, too.

"Lose your job." Walter's scowling, probably figuring he'll never get the extra dough out of me now. "What? What you do again? *Bippers?*"

"*Beepers.*"

"*Bippers.* Sandwiches."

"That's Blimpy's. *Beepers,* Walter. Pagers."

He's got his head jutting out at me, moose-style, frowning, his nose hitched up into his forehead. He's silent for a spell and for one brief, shining moment, I think—I'm not sure, but I think—he actually feels sorry for me. He crams his fingers under the rancid latex of his toupee, addresses an itch in the nape of his neck (probably head lice), and looks at me.

CHYNA

"I pay you to wrestle. You're not ready, but I make you wrestle anyway."

"What?" I'm not sure what I heard.

"I think he said he'd pay you to wrestle," Dan offers.

"Him." Walter points at Dan, nodding. "What he says. I pay you to wrestle . . . okay?"

FUCK, YEAH!

■ ■ ■

Independent wrestling leagues were the backbone of big-time pro wrestling. Ohio, Indiana, Tennessee—all these loose confederacies provided entertainment for middle America. That's where it all started, really. Jerry Lawler, our ring commentator, owned a fairly large league in Memphis for quite some time. It was even televised on a local affiliate. Vince McMahon and his father began buying up the small leagues, along with their talent, to eventually create the empire that gives you *Raw Is War, SmackDown!,* and, coming soon to a stadium near you, the XFL—extreme football.

But most of these independent leagues were cheesy folding-chair shows, usually held in high school gyms or VFW halls. The promoter charges maybe five bucks, pumps in a little Whitesnake or Poison, and pays his nieces and nephews minimum wage to sell the concessions. Like nachos, with

CHYNA *Wrestling Is Fake*

cheese that comes in big ole coffee cans that he could buy in bulk at the Food Warehouse, and soda—partial-fills he could get at the docks of the local bottling company. In that, er, no-man's-land before the WWF hired me, I worked the independents—Moolah, the legendary female wrestler from the forties and fifties, had one; Liz Chase did, too, among others. The talent should really be called something else. You don't wrestle, you throw people around. Some fat chick sits on your head and thinks your skull is made of stone. Hers seems to be, anyway. You get hurt a lot more wrestling in the independents because the skill is at "see level." If you're in the audience, you see all the fake punches, the fake kicks that don't connect, the real blood when someone accidentally does connect. And the costumes! Red flannel tights. Dog collars. Lots of Marilyn Monroe wigs. Glitter and football eye-black. Sometimes you drive for five hours to make twenty-five bucks. The promoters pay you in a back room, and sometimes

CHYNA

they won't pay you at all. Threaten them and you'll never get the chance to be stiffed again. Checks bounce. Once I had to sell my spare tire for gas. But it wasn't about the money. We would've all done it for free, and all of us did the independents — Hunter, Kane, Mick, Undertaker, Stone Cold, Billy, everyone paid the same kind of shitty dues. So when Walter told me that day that he would pay me to wrestle in one of his shows, well, I *flew* home. At least I think I did, because I don't remember driving. Boys and girls, a dream had been brought to life! A wish had been answered. Sure, I broke my tailbone on his fucking hard floor, but wishbone, tailbone, who's complaining? I was gonna wrestle for thirty bucks! Oh, my God, I don't have a thing to wear . . .

Marshall's. I high-tailed it to Marshall's, bought this pink bathing suit on sale, and got another 10 percent off because it had a tiny grease spot on the left butt cheek. At the fabric store I bought bags of glitter and a couple of yards of stretch lining, sewed the whole mess around the middle of the bathing suit so I had this glittery waistband. And I bought these terrific ivory-colored stockings. The afternoon before the match, which was an hour-and-a-half drive over to Worcester, I did my hair, at the time a shade best described as crabapple, blew it dry, fashioned it, hated it, washed it again, and started all over, finally getting the

CHYNA

pageboy I wanted without some of the ends flipping the other way like busted guitar strings. Then I dressed and studied myself in the mirror. As I recall, I looked like a ballerina in a porno movie, but at the time I thought, "Yeah! Apple pie. I am apple pie." Started talking to my imaginary opponent. "Hey, bitch. Yeah, you. C'mere and get your spanking. Huh? What'd you call me, bitch? POSER. You wanna call me something? Start with Lawry's. 'Cause I'm gonna pepper your bubble-ass and beat the ugly into your face. I am gonna *tenderize* you like a chicken, pretty lady. Girl. GIRLIE, GIRL."

■ ■ ■

"What the hell, Walter," I kept saying. "What the hell." It was ten minutes before my match and he was preparing my opponent, this 180-pound *man*. "What the hell, Walter—I thought I was gonna wrestle a chick?"

"You are," Walter insists, stuffing fake breasts inside this poor guy's leotard.

"A real chick. You said a real chick."

"Never used the word real. I couldn't book anybody this late."

"But he has stubble, Walter—" Before I could finish Walter shoves this bizarre-looking latex mask in my face. It's for the guy to wear.

CHINA *Wrestling Is Fake*

"Okay? Nobody's gonna know. You wrestle him, you'll learn something. He's good with flips, very quick, runs around the ring a lot, makes everything look smooth."

Sure, it would've been easier on both of us to just wrestle man against woman. But this was early on and in the independents, where you wrestled in places like the local AFL-CIO headquarters, the Knights of Columbus hall, or the Fin, Fur, and Feather clubhouse; the only place people wanted to see a woman compete against a man was in a chili cook-off or on *Jeopardy!* Guys just didn't smack the ladies around; they saved that for the home. Also, we're talking about '94, '95, which, in the grand cultural scheme of things, wasn't a high point in terms of how shocking we could all get. Springer, Howard Stern, reality shows, MTV's *Real World,* "America's Most Botched Circumcisions"—these forms of entertainment were pretty much in their infancy. And for better or worse, as they caught on and led to *Survivor, Big Brother,* or even some chick flashing her tits at Katie Couric on network TV, they made it a little easier for me to wrestle men in the WWF. But at the time of that thirty-dollar match, well, dare-to-be-different wasn't gonna play just yet.

"Okay, okay," I said to Walter, "I'll wrestle, I'll wrestle. Who wins?"

"You. Just make sure not to body-slam him and make his boobies go funny."

And so I fought my first match for money in front of forty people, and it was good. My match partner turned out to be cooperative and obliging and Walter had us fight each other another three or four times in the indies. Oh, yeah—his name was Raindrops. Don't ask.

8

Only the
Strong Survive

Rena? Dead! Gorgeous George?

Dead! Sunny and Nicole? DEAD AND DEADER! Madusa? DEAD!! Asya? *DEAAAAAAAD!!!!*

Sorry, sorry, I'm back now, I'm . . . better. It's just that every once in a while, I get a little emotional. Listen, in this business? You see so many women come and go. Everybody and their aunt can wrestle, right? Stanslavski school of wrestling. You dig deep, think about the last time your girl-friend dissed you for the shirt you were wearing or the room-mate who used your twenty-dollar shampoo to clean the upholstery on her piece-of-shit Corolla, and presto, you're mean as Triple H on Preparation H or you're Stephanie McMahon after she's watched a Memorial Day *Dallas* marathon—a little attitude goes a long way, right? And, hey, the mat kind of . . . *bounces*. Doesn't look any harder than a queen-size double at the Sunset Boulevard Kiss-and-Tell. Wrong. All the bouncing does is make sure you get hit twice, from the backlash. And to be in this business you need car-bonated hope in a bottle, you need the Martin Luther King "I have a dream" speech playing in your head from the minute your bleary eyes open to the moment your mat-burned tem-ple hits the pillow. To be *successful* in this business you need all that times ten—you need the heart of a lion.

I've been here a while, so now it's my turn to show the

CHYNA

new girls around. Nine times out of ten, you hear the same thing: "Where can I put my makeup on?" Are you kidding me? Girl, this is a sweatshop, a good old-fashioned tights version of conveyor-belt capitalism. People see a gleaming, sleek luxury car called *Smackdown!*, but if they saw the bolts going in, well, that's another trip entirely—maybe that course in cosmetology over at Saddleback doesn't look so bad after all. I mean, a job at McDonald's—you could end up facedown on the floor in the freezer, but at least you get a break on your food. Here, you better have the best frigging luggage money can buy, and if you're not into hotel floral prints, forget about it.

Jackie, Debra, Terry, Lita came in—very respectful, kept their heads down, learned the ropes, literally, and found it within themselves to stay out of the way without getting lost in the shuffle. I don't mind taking credit for making it a little easier on them because, hopefully, they'll be doing the same one day—pass on a little compassion for the new meat. But when I came in? Resistance. Anger. Suspicion. Ridicule. Jealousy. Sexual harassment. Worst of all? Fraud. Pure and simple, out-and-out phony, bullshit-slinging, honey-you're-gonna-go-far fucking fraud. Yeah, well, I knew a few things about doing the I-ain't-who-I-say-I-am waltz, I knew a little about getting the real lowdown. Part of my best schooling in

CHYNA *Only the Strong Survive*

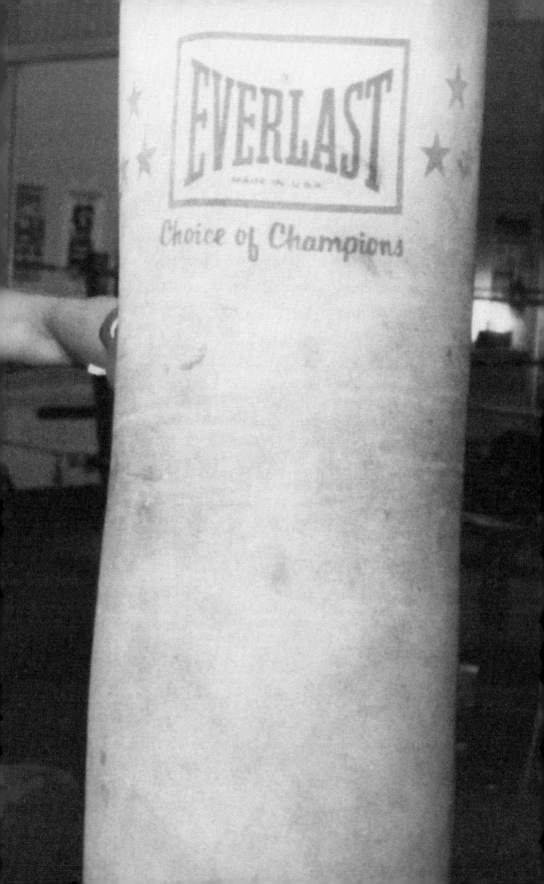

matters of information-gathering and recon—remember, I interviewed with the Secret Service—came from a woman we'll call Beverly.

Bev was a ring rat, a groupie—I suppose the more blatant term would be star-fucker—but Bev was so much more than that. Bev *fucked* with the stars; Bev fucked with everyone. Bev had this check-writing system (like me, she usually didn't have money for toilet paper) that was unparalleled. She'd write one, time it, make deposits to time when the checks would have to clear; I mean she juggled, baby, she juggled. Most of all, Bev loved wrestling. Like Hunter and Mick Foley, she was a walking encyclopedia of wrestling history and factoids—who held the Southwestern Tennessee Valley extreme belt in 1982 or who pinned The Sheik in Tokyo back in '66. And, working independent shows, she networked like nobody's business. Everyone knew Bev, and for a while, she kind of hip-pocket managed me—turned me on to shows, let me know who was in town, where they were looking for chick wrestlers, that sort of thing. She had an ongoing sleepage thing with this WWF agent. He'd beep her when the WWF was in town (she lived at the time in West Palm Beach), they'd get together for a bottle of wine and a few submission holds, and during the ensuing pillow talk, the guy—we'll call him Agent Orange—would give her the inside skinny.

CHYNA

Things in the WWF
get hot at times.

The beginning of Mick Foley's
attraction to Chyna.

When I started at the
WWF I was a woman
standing alone.

Imitation is the
sincerest form
of flattery.

Power.
Beauty.
Strength.

A seven-year-old Joanie . . . still smiling.

◀ **H**at and slippers by Grandma. Smile by Joanie.

◀ **M**y sister, Kathy, and I — best friends always.

▶ **K**athy lending me support at the Fitness America Pageant.

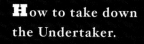

How to take down
the Undertaker.

Hunter and Chyna.

◀ **S**mell this, Rock!

◀ **E**very relationship has its ups and downs. Chyna with Eddie Guerrero.

▶ **C**hyna Fitness . . . More Than Meets the Eye.

Typical DX.

...I did it for me.

One afternoon I was crying my eyes out over the fact that, one, some asshole in my last independent show asked me if I had a dick; two, my boyfriend is a loser; and three, the carpet still smells like dog piss, when the phone rang.

"They're coming to Springfield, Joanie! The WWF! In Springfield!" Bev was ecstatic. "And I talked to my agent friend. He said he'd meet with you, Joanie!"

"When? When?"

"Tonight! The show's tonight! He'll leave you a ticket at will-call. Bring *everything*—your videos, photos, bio, pamphlets, the works. Sell this tool, Joan."

No problem. As long as I drove about 150 miles an hour. Springfield, Massachusetts, was at least three and a half hours away. The show began at 7:30 and it was already four P.M. If I took a quick shower, dried my hair by car window, and put my makeup on behind the wheel, I might make it. Naturally, I had wrestled that day in school and this woman-hating poser that Walter was pushing as the next Hulk Hogan had worked his elbow into my thigh for maximum lift trying to throw me. Most guys always felt they had something to prove by beating the crap out of me. I had put the dog down, no problem, but now I had a bruise the size of a tostada on my leg, and worse, a charley horse that made it nearly impossible to walk without pain. I mean, this was one time—one time—where I just wanted to guzzle a half-bottle of Nyquil, crawl into bed, and

Only the Strong Survive

dream about being a pro wrestler. "Go go go go. Do it, do it, do it, do it," I had to tell myself. Walking to the car, I was limping noticeably.

By the time I rolled into Springfield it was nearly dark; I recall finding a hydrant where no one had parked, which boded well, luckwise. It was an omen. I figured that paying the ticket would beat having to walk half a mile or so on a bad wheel. How bad was it? After sitting in the car that long, I climbed out of the seat, fell down from the stiffness, and ripped a hole in my panty hose. Nice. But I made it before the first match and found my seat, which was another good sign: It was a great seat, near the ring. Time for the first match: Take it all in, Joanie, take it all in, I told myself when the lights went down and the crowd went up like a Texas-size beehive. Oh, it was glorious, and soon it was gonna be all mine. Soon . . .

Fourth match of the night: British Bull Dog vs. The Dentist (now Kane). No sign of Agent Orange. Intermission

came and went. I really had to pee, too, but I was afraid that if I left my seat, I might miss him. Second-to-last match—a six-man tag-team deal—no Orange. Last match of the night—Undertaker and Stone Cold Steve Austin. Now, normally, I would be riveted to a match like that—Stone Cold was becoming a real crowd favorite then, a real Everyman kind of wrestler, with his funky muscle cars and his Budweiser. And Undertaker, I mean, so graceful for a big man. At that time, I never would have guessed he would be someone I would confide in many times. He's just as graceful a human being! But tonight it was just sad. Sad, because I had been abandoned, jammed, bullshitted by this Agent Orange prick. Probably spotted some rat in bang-me mules and a SUCK IT! T-shirt and just couldn't resist. By the time the ring crew started to dismantle everything, I was ready to do the same to him. Great seat, yeah, sure. A better one at this point would've been on his lying face. But I sat there and waited.

"Ma'am," this security guard says, "you have to leave."

"Can you give me just a little more time? I think the guy I'm waiting for is with some of the wrestlers."

"Sorry." He motioned with his hand for me to get up. He's escorting me out of the building. "What you got there? Autograph book?" he asked about my portfolio. I wanted to smash him over the head with it, but that would've been

CHYNA

classic aggression transfer (I wanted to save my armaments for Orange), and besides, my charley horse was killing me.

Parking lot. Dark, empty. Across the street I can see my car, with a stiff ticket tucked under the wipers, fluttering in the New England wind. Orange-colored. Bastard. I felt cut loose in deep space, I felt cheated, I felt ashamed because I allowed myself to be suckered into believing I was in for a beautiful night. And then it hit me. The Agent? He was meaningless. I conned myself. I was the one responsible for driving three and a half hours at speeds approaching ninety while putting on my makeup and eating a three-pound cheese pizza from Sal's. I was the one with the power to fool me . . . I WAS THE ONE WITH THE POWER.

There was a concession guy still packing up near the loading docks.

"Listen," I said, "I'm looking for a guy, he works for the WWF, his name is Agent Orange?" The guy knew who he was, smiled. "Right, right," he said, "sure, Agent Orange — the dude with the Michael Bolton hair extensions." Another guy named Dave Hebner joined him and listened.

"That's him! Well, I need to find him immediately," I lied. "Our mother is on dialysis, and she needs one of his kidneys. Please! Please tell me where I can find him!"

At that point, I thought all three of us were gonna pee

in the street together—me because I really had to go, and the fellas because they were laughing so hard at my story. But I got what I wanted—sort of. They told me Agent Orange had left about an hour ago. He was staying at the Holiday Inn in Hartford, Connecticut—another half-hour away, in the wrong direction from my hovel. And it was one in the morning.

I left the fire hydrant ticket between the wipers—something to focus on.

1:45 A.M., Holiday Inn, Hartford, Connecticut

"Hello, Agent Orange?"

"Yeah." He sounded all raspy and addled on the phone. Agent Orange had probably ordered a little room service, got down to the Bailey's Irish Cream in the mini-bar, and channel-surfed through the adult movies on SpectraVision until he fell asleep.

"Hi, my name is Joanie Laurer?"

"Well, hello . . ." He seemed to perk up. Mainly because he didn't remember who I was until I reminded him.

"You were supposed to meet me at the arena tonight?"

"Oh, oh . . . jeez, I'm sorry—was that for tonight? I thought—"

"Listen," I said, "why don't you come down and at least have a beer or something with me at the bar? I drove a long way to see you. Can you do that for me at least?"

About a half-hour later, we're having coffee. I am, anyway, and I'm showing him news clippings, photos, a kind of Joanie Laurer–in–pictures tour. Agent Orange's eyes keep fluttering; he's nodding off when one of my photos gets a pulse.

"What happened to her?" He's pointing at a photo of this girl I wrestled, her name is Angie. The picture was snapped not long after I had broken her nose. The fabulous Moolah, a legend in women's wrestling, had set up one of my earliest matches as an independent. I was wrestling as Joanie Lee at the time. This is how far wrestling's come since then: Angie and this guy named Thumper were paired against me and Buddy Valentine in a tag-team match. But the girls were only allowed to fight against the girls and the guys against the guys. I really had this inclination to go after Thumper because I had a bad feeling about Angie, she was so small compared to me. Before the match, Angie and I practiced this full-nelson work, with Angie applying it to me, locking both my arms behind my head. During the match, things didn't go as smoothly. Angie gets me in the hold, I jerk my hands down to break out of it and she's supposed to immediately let go—only she didn't, she held on, which yanked her forward, her nose going smack into the back of my head. I remember the sound, too, kind of like someone shaking the buckshot in a shotgun shell. I turned around and, my God, there was blood everywhere. Angie's face was pretty much destroyed. To her credit, she signaled for me to feed on it, make it a big deal. I did this big ole dramatic super-glare, the don't-fuck-with-me glare that Stone Cold is probably the best at doing. The crowd ate it up, but after the match I just felt like crawling in a hole, I felt so bad for Angie . . .

I look over and Agent Orange is receiving nocturnal communion—got his tongue out, head back, sound asleep. Now I *am* gonna hit him. That's it. I'm gonna mop the floor with this guy's face and drive home, the memory of mopping the floor with this guy's face enough to keep me awake for what is now a four-hour drive. You know why he got out of bed? To get his dick wet. You know why he was sleeping now? Because I was here for a job, I'm here because I want to wrestle, I'm here for the love of the sport. "SOL," my friend Luna always says, referring to women in wrestling. "We're Shit-out-of-luck. We're not strippers. We're not bimbos, we're not empty-headed females. We like the sport. We love to entertain. We didn't want to be in this sport to be close to men—we got in this sport because we love wrestling. But SOL, baby. You know what the men have done to us? Besides paying us tons less than the men,

CHYNA

objectifying us into eye candy, T&A, the little wet dream for the little weenies? They turned us on each other. SOL. Made us back-stab each other, turned us into being nasty to each other instead of lifting each other up. And the real bitch is you try and get tough? You try to get beyond the girlie thing, you show 'em you're into the moves and counter-moves and that you can take a dive off the top rope as good as any of them, they start calling you a man, a dyke, a 'roid junkie, a muffin diver, all that crap. SOL, Joanie, SOL." 'Roid junkie—steroid user. I got that a lot, as you can well imagine. Heaven forbid I did it on my own, with sweat and hard work. 'Roid junkie, SOL. As long as I am fit, I will always get it: SOL.

Agent Orange starts to stir. Wakey, wakey, little fella. But as he's coming to, he waves. Not to me, but to Hunter, Sean Michaels, and Stone Cold, who had just walked in. Now, you have to remember, this is the first time I've met Hunter, my right leg has no feeling in it, and just a few hours ago, I may've been about as close to slashing my wrists as I've ever been. So I was seeing this man, Paul Levesque, through a prism of shit. I mean, there was every reason to lump him into the Man Heap, of Guys with Angles. He did something with his eyes, though—it wasn't a look, or a come-on, or a blow-off. They clicked just slightly, left to right, and his lips moved without him saying

CHYNA *Only the Strong Survive*

anything, then he nodded at me—the whole thing took less than a heartbeat and it occurred *after* the introductions, the "Joanie, this is Hunter, Hunter, this is Joanie." It was like in that instant he knew what my deal was, where I was coming from, that you had to look a long, long way to see through me (It's not vanity, either. I know I'm complicated and it's a handicap, okay?)—he figured me out and decided it was cool. Looking back on it, it's easier for me to understand it now—Hunter is heavy into first impressions. With him, it's like a meteor coming close to the earth. Something's either gonna hit and leave a huge dent or miss completely, then and there. Not that he wasn't cute. Had that incredible hairline, the stare of a Roman general, smart, *driven*. But he had this good-guy, raised-on-a-farm quality (he wasn't at all, which made him all the more cool).

"You trained with Walter Kowalski," I said. "So did I."

"Oh, God, you poor thing. 'GODDAMMIT, YOU STUPID *EEDIOT*, WHAT'S THE MATTER WITH YOU? EVERYBODY GO HOME!' Walter, right? Walter's okay. He's just such a goddamn cheapskate. You break your tailbone yet?"

"I did." I was laughing now.

"Yup. Yup. Son of a bitch won't pop for a new ring. Never will." We were both wrong—one month after I left Walter's he got a brand-new ring! "When I was there, he

had two-by-fours over plywood. The two-by-fours kept snapping, so he replaced them with steel beams. Nice. Body-slamming on concrete is softer."

"'You, Joan *Lair*,'" I said in my best Polish accent, "'you can't work for anybody! Not while you're in my school!'" We were riffing on Walter-isms. The thing about Walter was that he knew everybody, because he wrestled in the dark ages—against Dick the Bruiser, Haystack Calhoun, Bruno Sammartino—and with the school (really, it was one of the first "serious" wrestling schools), he managed to stay relevant and ran a lot of young talent through his place. Vince McMahon hired Walter early on, before the school but after Walter applied his last claw hold to an opponent's throat and started using it to open marshmallow topping. Vince had a soft spot for Walter; in fact, Vince helped a lot of the old guys. Walter's job was to cross off the matches on a sheet of paper after each one happened.

"Yeah." Hunter laughed. "And if anyone could find a way to screw that up it would be Walter."

Around 2:30, Agent Orange went back to bed. The notion that he'd actually done something for someone without getting paid or laid for it probably made it hard for him to get back to sleep, thinking he was slipping. Sigh.

Hunter and Sean invited me up to their room—the bar was closing—where they checked out my portfolio. Yeah,

CHYNA *Only the Strong Survive*

sounds weird when I say it, too, but it was true and I was only doing what both of them—especially Hunter—had done when they first tried to break into the business. Both of them were sweet and very gracious about paging through a mountain of photos, pictures, and articles from muscle magazines I'd put together—the big metamorphosis from Joanie Lee to nose-breaker to Kowalski victim. It was truly one of those Mary Tyler Moore–Holly Golightly moments, had they been written by David Lynch. A woman with ambition, taking her portfolio around Manhattan, showing off her photo shoots, wearing Manolo Blahnik pumps and schmoozing in the lobby of the Royalton—except it's me, at the Holiday Inn, and I'm sweating through my clothes, showing snapshots to a couple of strangers. Hunter and Sean popped this compilation tape I made into the VCR—boxing, lifting, some wrestling matches. They'd pretty much seen it all before and, as I say, they were gracious about sitting through it—until they reached Bad Brad.

Now Bad Brad had a formidable reputation on the independent circuit—a real cult following with the folding-chair and black-velveteen-curtains set. A loyal Tarheel, born in North Carolina, Bad Brad would do anything to get in the ring with someone. Guys on the way up would use him in the same way the Harlem Globetrotters always trounced the Washington Generals. I backed the tape with

CHYNA

that LL Cool J tune "Mama Said Knock You Out" and some White Zombie tracks. The music seemed to energize the two of them, gave the night a little kick in the butt to get us over the top. But the part that seemed to make them slide to the edge of their seats, the piece that sealed it for them—i.e., the lady has an engine ID number, she's got papers, the girl has a pedigree, the woman needs a shot to shine—was me taking out Bad Brad. Toward the end of the match, he knocks me down with a haymaker, then, tired of having me kick his ass all night—me, this wound-up, crazy Hannibal bitch—he finds a folding chair. In pro wrestling, the folding chair is like the doorbell in a sitcom or the cape in a bullfight. It's a costar, really, opens up all kinds of deliciously vicious possibilities. And how you handle it reveals almost as much about your skill and ability as being able to body-slam, arm-smash, or take a fall. Most people don't walk through life getting hit with a folding chair, so most people don't know what it's really supposed to look or feel like. Hitting somebody with it, you wind up, you grunt, you put your whole body into it. It's kind of like throwing a change-up in baseball—you sell it in the windup and then feel the momentum. The recipient does get hit, and usually pretty good, too!

So Hunter and Sean are watching Bad Brad come at me with this folding chair, but I spring to my feet and drop-kick the chair, which hits Bad Brad square in the face. Not only that, but I kicked *through* the chair—the momentum thing—I take Bad Brad's head off with it. He was bloody, but it just looked terrific; Hunter and Sean are cheerleading, hooting, pointing at the set, really into it. Hunter rewound the tape over and over, laughing his ass off!

"You know something, we could maybe use her as a bodyguard"—Hunter's wound-up, scheming, speed-talking now—"like, wouldn't it be cool if she was kicking guys' asses as a bodyguard, just be this killer bone-crusher woman?"

"Yeah. And she's hot, too. Most built women are heinous, but she's pretty." Sean's talking to Hunter, Hunter's riffing off Sean—it's nearing dawn and it's like I'm not in the room anymore. After about fifty minutes of this—and I'm not complaining, trust me, I am speechless anyway, I am so high I piggy-backed on the rising sun—Sean asked me if I wanted to stay. Not like that, not like that, okay? And that also helped. That these guys were serious enough to pay for my own room for me so I wouldn't have to make the long drive. As wasted as I was, I wanted to go—not because I didn't trust them, or was afraid one of them might make that signature male midnight creep, that I'd wake up again with someone's dick in my hand. These guys were serious and respectful—all business, even to the point where Hunter, getting himself a glass of water,

chugs it down, then just stands there, looking at me while we're shaking hands good-bye. Does that thing again, with the click in his eyes and the meditative nod.

"Can we keep these for a while?" Sean asks, referring to my portfolio. I am maybe higher than I'd ever been before, in terms of the feel-good movie of the year. I was Bambi, discovering that I could stand. I was all *Matrix*-y and inspired. I got in, damn it, they let me in.

"Keep them as long as you like," I think I said, but Hunter didn't wait for me to finish.

"I'm gonna get into this today. But you need to know something. We do this, we're taking sort of a shot here. Both of us, me and Sean, you know? Because there are a lot of people trying to break into this business. You get up on someone, especially being that you're a woman, help them out, then discover they're irresponsible, totally on drugs, psycho and worse. So . . ."

I made some noise about not being any of those things (so I lied about the psycho) and reverently bowed, thanked them three or four times, shook hands with each of them twice, then drove home reborn, energized, fucking happy as a goddess slumming—it was one of the truly fantastic moments of my sugar-free short life. And I remember being on the freeway in Hartford, seeing all the unsmiling

Only the Strong Survive

people in a big gray line of traffic headed off to work and feeling sorry for them, but being so glad I was out of a job, because wrestling wasn't gonna be a job, or an adventure, or a love affair, or a calling—it was gonna be my life, and finally, finally, Joanie was gonna start living. I was in!

"N-O. No. No, and hell, no," Vince McMahon answered, when Hunter and Sean approached him about me. In fact, according to Hunter, who 'fessed up some time well after I was hired, Vince hated the idea. "She's never really worked anywhere. What if she's a flake? And what's a woman gonna do, beat up the guys? No one's gonna go for that. She's gonna hit guys?"

"Well, yeah, Vince. Just think about it—it's never been done before, except for these monster women who looked like freaks," Hunter argued. "She's hot. And we start her out easy. Maybe she doesn't hit anybody right off—"

"I personally have no interest in seeing a big woman ass-kicker," Vince resisted. You have to remember that Vince was a fifty-year-old man and he didn't necessarily see what everybody else thought was cool. He looked at the business in a different way and, frankly, that was the knock on the WWF at the time—it was a little, well, stodgy.

"Vince, Vince, Vince—you gotta see this movie, *Double Impact,* with Van Damme. There's this female body builder,

CHYNA

Corey Everson. She's a lot smaller than our girl, and she plays a bodyguard—she's the heavy and she beats everybody up. It worked great! She kicked Van Damme's ass and everybody bought it." The movie—Hunter and Sean kept going back to that movie, hammering it home that it worked. But Vince wasn't buying it.

"Forget it. Not gonna happen. Okay, so she hits a guy. What then? The guy's gonna hit her back? Unh-uh. No one's gonna work with her. No one's gonna sell her, it's taboo. And if they even did, who's gonna want to allow themselves to get beat up by a woman?"

The guys kept working on Vince, but he had a very powerful argument. What he said cut to the very marrow of what the ring is all about. Wrestlers are like bookies. We all are, we make our living on the vigorish. Most people have to cheer for either the good guy or the bad guy—it always comes down to that. Eventually, you have to be on one side or the other. As wrestlers, we want our bad guys to be reviled and hated as much as the good guys are loved and revered. The real, true-blooded, honest-to-God people in our business, the best of us? We don't care who wins or loses or even how the game is played. We want a pulse—that's our vig. We want life, and life is what happens long before the verdict comes in, long before the ref slaps the mat. Sure, wrestling is fake:

CHYNA

The violence we visit upon each other comes in the form of waiting, uncertainty, and devoting yourself to achieving stardom in a world that is essentially false, at the expense of those close to you, at the expense of those you seek out for comfort. It's the grand ole opry. People liken it to soap operas, but the range of emotion is much narrower, at least what you see on the screen—winners, losers. Hate, love. Extremes. Nothing subtle—someone wins, someone loses. In between is what we live with, what we do. You want a reaction, you want a pulse. When there's none, you're in big, big trouble. You may as well be paired up with a toll-booth attendant—I mean, they'll break something, even if it is a five-dollar bill. The truth of the matter is that to wrestle requires agility, strength, and most of all, cooperation.

■ ■ ■

So Vince was right. And, frankly, even after he hired me, he *still* was right. I had a tough, tough time with a few of the guys. I remember one big Pay-Per-View, my opponent was supposed to be the heel—the bad guy. But he didn't want to be. He wouldn't be there for me, he wouldn't be the heel, the complete asshole I needed him to be—and therefore became an asshole in real life. I remember looking at him in the ring that night and I almost lost it, I almost wanted to shoot-wrestle, just to see what I could force out of him. He had this

expression that little kids in training pants get when the poopie gets so thick it starts coming out of the sides. He vacillated between disdain and boredom. Congratulations, asshole, you just won a lifetime subscription to *Plant Life* magazine. And there were others, too, who just couldn't get behind the idea of Chyna, woman, beating so-and-so, man. Weird. It boiled down to some twisted life view/sex myth: Women can't fight because men refuse to fake it.

Well, here, let Jericho put it in his own words (if you could see him, he'd be flipping his hair):

Ah, Chyna, my Chyna. She's definitely more than just this body art. She became kind of the symbol of the—I don't know if it's the symbol of women's lib, but definitely in wrestling, because before women, most women in this business—

What? "Before women, most women . . ." What the hell is the chucklehead saying?

—I'm saying, lady, that most women in this business were either T&A or they were wrestling against other women so they didn't really have too much involvement with the guys. In my opinion,

CHYNA

women's wrestling is kind of dead in the States almost. In Japan, it's awesome, because the women are kind of porky, chubby lesbian girls who kick the shit out of each other and it's kind of fun to watch.

Couldn't have said it better myself. What a charmer, eh?

But I'm getting way ahead of myself, here. So Hunter and Sean Michaels pitched me to Vince and he threw it up like the little girl with the pea soup. He *hated* it.

"We talked to Vince and he's mulling it over," Hunter told me a few weeks later.

9

The Good Girl Always Wins

My body. Muscle definition leading up to places undeniably feminine, like a lit-up runway for planes to land on. I have Big Jessica Rabbit Beauty covering a heart that won't stop longing for the little things. Smooth and hard, tall as a flagpole, and I am flying my freak flag high, as the man who wrote "Foxy Lady" liked to say. So there it is in the full-length mirror when I wake, there it is in the eyes of admirers and detractors, there it is, splashed across the pages of *Talk* magazine in chronological cells—a history of conspicuousness. Half feminine, half power bomb. Me and my body, Joanie and Chyna. A load, isn't it? It's that car with all the fins, the skyscraper among the high-rises, the wineglass when everyone else is drinking out of mugs—and I wouldn't have it any other way. Honestly, the love affair I have with my body began early on. It just took me a while to go public with it. Around the time change came in convulsions for me, when whole chunks of my previous life were falling away on a daily basis—you could call that early-morning drive home from Hartford my point of no return—I had a chance, once and for all, to throw down, become my own woman.

Tribeca Theater, Manhattan: The Deuce is here! ESPN2 is covering the Fitness America Competition and how cool is that? The camera pans across the stage, dis-

playing each contestant in all her tanned, toned, trim, petite glory: The brunette psych major from Ohio State, 105 pounds. A policewoman from New Jersey, got the two-piece Danskin and the cute little book-'em-Dano, isosceles gun stance, tipping the scales at 114. Then the chick from Louisville, cool as a mint julep and wearing bright white ankle socks, screen graphic: 106 pounds. A real estate agent, the token brick shithouse at 135 pounds; the twenty-three-year old from Salem, Oregon, wearing a scarf around her neck (I like that), 119 pounds; the camera panning, panning, kitten after kitten, all smiles all the time, until it settles on little ole me. I can see myself on the monitors to the left and right of us. I look positively otherworldly and 100 percent out of place in my belly-dancing costume, my hands rakishly propping the sword out in front of me like Gene Kelly with a cane. The screen graphic: Joan Laurer, Lowell, Massachusetts, 150 pounds. I weighed closer to 165, but the assholes refused to accept that number when I wrote it down on my application. They had their reasons, but the camera doesn't lie. The cameraman has a sense of humor, too. He backs off for this medium shot to get me in with the other girls. It looks like a kiddie line for a Saturday matinee until you get to me: "Sorry, miss, but you definitely look over twelve years old."

I had been at war with the Fitness America people for maybe two years. If you dream of becoming an actress, a star,

The Good Girl Always Wins

a celebrity, Fitness America is the end of the line, baby, your last-ditch effort to get some exposure. After that, there's miming in the West Village. And with a body like mine, you can forget cattle calls for extras. "Uh, yeah, we're, um, doing this music video for Creed and we need as many 180-pound, five-foot-ten women as you can find." What makes the Fitness America pageant so perfect is you pay your entrance fee and you're in. I've competed in three and finished dead last every time. I was always a crowd pleaser, though. The other girls would put some techno-pop on, do jumping jacks so their giant tits would bounce, segue into leg lifts, push-ups, the kind of stuff you see on cable TV at eight in the morning or very late at night on the pay channel. I always tried something wacky; one time I danced the twist. Same result—last place. It was a beauty pageant, pure and sim-ple—girls in bikinis who would probably get winded chang-ing lanes on the freeway. I mean, they weren't fit. They were the typical American beauty queens. Only now they were supposedly fit as well.

Like I said, you pay your entrance fee, show up, and you're in. They can't turn you down, no matter how many times you've entered. Not that they didn't try. After losing my last one, I got this letter, informing me that Fitness America was just that, a fitness pageant, and with my "particular skills" perhaps I would be better served entering bodybuilding com-

petitions. They even provided a list. They were pretty much asking me not to come anymore and, naturally, at first I was crushed. In my own Joanie psychodrama, I imagined them composing the letter, passing it around the office, getting together in little discussion groups to rip on me. I imagined all those I ever competed against, the Gidgets of this earth with their false gentility, all getting a *copy* of the letter and showing it to their friends. And for a long time I felt beaten— you know, they're not gonna have Joanie Laurer to kick around anymore. But Fitness America pushed another button, too, with that letter. Perhaps I would be better served entering bodybuilding competitions? *Bodybuilding competitions?* If the insensitive, mother-fucking, genteel, form-letter-sending, white-shoe-and-carnation-wearing assholes only knew. Oh, I tried a bodybuilding competition, all right. Tried it just once.

Back in my Key West, three-legged-dog days, one of my best friends worked in a gym. Suzy Schaf talked to animals. I did, too, but as an animal activist who majored in zoology, she spoke to real ones, got involved in every animal-rights cause, as in save the you-fill-in-the-blank. In the Great War of Survival, she was, as they say, in the next foxhole over. Suzy was there for me when the bombs went off. Picked me up from the hospital after the drunk driver played chiropractor to my face, took me home, took a picture of me

CHYNA

with my face as purple as a grape. We were driving to a bar one night to celebrate, drinks on me because I had finally left Tom and his faithful dog, Shitter.

"Joanie," she said as she pointed, "isn't that where you're waitressing?" The place was surrounded by fire trucks; it had burned to the ground. "When I think I'm having a bad day, I just think of your luck," she used to say.

Suzy had a petite body—no breasts, flat as checker-board—but she worked out and looked terrific. We met working part-time at the Paradise Gym, which was anything but. To give you an idea of how thoroughly behind the times the Paradise was, the exercise bikes were actual Schwinns with their rear tires elevated—if you were in the Paradise, you weren't going anywhere. So when Suzy told me she entered this bodybuilding contest, I was happy for her.

"You could do it, too," she suggested one day. "The way your body responds, you'd do great." But I didn't know the first thing about it. You needed to have muscles that looked like they had a life of their own, that much I knew. And it wasn't for the shy or retiring. The ones I'd seen on TV, the girls wore just enough to cover the quarters and the coin return, know what I'm sayin'?

"Look," Sue told me, "you already have the work ethic. All you need to know is what and how to eat and how to paint."

The Good Girl Always Wins

"Paint? What the hell does painting have to do with bodybuilding?"

"Painting. *Tanning.* We use Pro Tan in the bottle. The muscles show up better on darker skin. Pigs have muscles."

"Pigs."

"Yeah, you know, bacon, ham. Pigs? Pigs have muscles, but you don't see them the way you can on, say, a rhinoceros because pigs are generally light-skinned."

Having not seen a rhinoceros since the last time I was with my mother, I had to take her word for it. "Can't we just use the tanning bed?"

"Bodybuilding is not as hard as you're making it out to be," Suzy said. "You got the hard part licked, Joanie. The hard part's the training. And we can push each other. Lisa competed, came in second." This was stunning news. I had seen Lisa just a few days ago—she worked at the dry cleaner's, and unless she was competing against Delta Burke, somebody stole second place. Lisa had highly developed fingers from writing all those dry-cleaning tickets. The rest of her was in need of some serious hemming. I mean this girl was all flab and gab.

And so we trained. And to make the train go choo-choo, you need the right fuel. The first thing you want to do is to make a complete mess out of your diet, your eating habits, and your appetite. In other words, you start eating healthy.

Chicken, broccoli, baked potatoes, and skinless tuna. Yum. And the baked potato, served naked as an albino moose turd—no bacon bits, no sour cream, no grated cheese, no butter, no I-Can't-Believe-It's-Not-Butter, no nothing— still, the baked potato is your junk food because you shouldn't even have that. They call it body sculpting, right? Well, that's not too far from the truth. You're working out every night, for two weeks straight, each night working on a different body part. Up to three days before competition, you're dropping fat and working out to the max to get those muscles to sprout. You're eating for fuel, to keep going while the exercise regimen planes those saddlebags right the hell off your hips. Three days before the match you go on an all-carbohydrate diet to put water into all that muscle mass you've shaped.

There are other things some contestants do, too, most of it illegal, dangerous, or both, like shooting up insulin, taking steroids, combining this drug with that to change your body chemistry. Insulin will change your blood sugar, for example, so that you can absorb more protein. The whole business is very complicated, sort of like growing a hothouse water-melon in five minutes, or mating a buffalo and a giraffe—at the end of the day it's not nice to fool with Mother Nature. And it's really all trial and error—too much of one thing and not enough of another can do dramatic things to your mood.

A day before the competition, Suzy and I are baking these special-recipe corn muffins called carbo surprise. You know you're in for a taste-bud jubilee when the apartment starts to smell like scented cat litter. But the muffins would have to do. As I said, a lot of body builders use health-threatening drugs and supplements. But not Suzy and me. We respected our bodies and understood the dangers of radically manipulating the metabolism with insulin and steroids. For Suzy, being a naturalist and into ecology, food chains, life cycles, animal preservation, and the natural order of things, nothing could be more sacrilegious than mainlining steroids and playing Dr. Frankenstein with your physique. She just couldn't do it on principle. Me? I had my own reasons. And not nearly as lofty, unless you consider keeping the president's hookers on the lowdown to be up there with restrictions on cloning and saving the wetlands. I wanted to be in the Secret Service. Oh, the dazzling, romantic life of a counteragent! Disguises, drug busts, fraud, money laundering. Living dangerously. Living on the edge. Having a false identity! An alter ego. And most of all, it wasn't a nine-to-five job. Yeah, sounds familiar to me, too. Sounds like I just described either the WWF or my father, agent double-oh-no.

You talk about an epic job interview—I'd been interviewing with the Secret Service for nearly a year. They have this elimination interview process, kind of like trying to get in the

CHYNA

hot seat for *Who Wants to Be a Millionaire?* At the time of the great corn-muffin bake-off, I was on my third go-round with them and someone even mentioned the eighteen-thousand-dollar-a-year entry-level salary. Today that wouldn't cover how much I spend on panty hose in a year, but back then you could've paid me *eight* dollars a year if it meant squirting Castro's beard with a poison pen or scamming some Chinese entrepreneur into selling me his bootleg Tears for Fears cassettes. So I slogged through the meetings, tests, background checks. These guys were thorough, as you can well imagine. If you so much as jaywalked in the middle of a magnitude-seven earthquake your chances of getting in were diminished. They want to know if you have a criminal record, extremist affiliations, unpaid parking tickets. They find out about overdue library books, tattoos. They look at your childhood, your scholastic history, your relatives (uh-oh). And the tests. *Hard.* I mean, I thought your job was to take a bullet for the First Family, not design a flak jacket. I took this memory-retention test a week before the body-building contest. This guy with a Gordon Liddy mustache hands me this picture, tells me to look at it for a moment, study it. It's a picture of a kitchen. Wow, right in my wheelhouse. I wonder if they give the male applicants a picture of the inside of a garage. After ten seconds, the Gordon Liddy wanna-be then takes it away from me. Starts asking me questions about it, but checks me out

The Good Girl Always Wins

because it's hot and I'm wearing a tube top (I had my ways of altering the curve a little on these things, if you catch my drift).

"How many cupboards were open?"

"Three," I answered correctly.

"How many cans of food were in the second cupboard?" he asked. I knew it was four. Then he wanted to know what was in the cans, the correct answer being beans.

"Why is there a handprint there?" he then asked, and that stumped me because damned if I saw a handprint anywhere, let alone what it was doing there.

"Sorry, I missed the handprint completely," I had to admit. "I just didn't see it in the picture."

"I mean on your shoulder. Looks like a handprint."

"Oh, that. That's from tanning stuff."

The Key West Body-Building Contest was a pretty big deal, actually. You know how local fanfare goes—Martha's Vineyard for music, Telluride for film, Key West for anything on the outer edge of culture. Sure, it had resorts and Hemingway's germs floating everywhere, but it was a magnet for bad taste. There were Key West Body Builder flyers in the supermarket, on bus stops, telephone poles. I saw one pinned up at a Starbucks and someone drew a cock on the woman in the flyer. The event would be staged at the Holiday Inn, which meant you wanted some green in your costume. The competition was held in one of those rank-

CHYNA

smelling conference rooms that give off an odor of cigarettes, rotten tangerines, and semen. Overhead lighting, like you're at the DMV. And lots of bunting. A stage made out of folding tables all lashed together, like we were all going upstream on a raft through Fantasy Island and there were all these smiling dwarf women with Naugahyde skin who were about to be sold into slavery to the highest bidder. At least that's the way it looked after my seventeenth corn muffin.

All my friends were there; Dad and his trinket-wife, Tina, showed. I was proud, I gotta say, and it looked like a cinch win for me. I was in the heavyweight division with just one other girl. I weighed in at 160; my competition weighed no more than 136, five-foot-eight, made the heavyweight division by one pound. Had her hair piled on top of her head like a poodle, wore a bikini that was a couple sizes too small for her, had big ole mozzarella balls swaying in that top, and her act was nearly as cheesy. She could claim not a single muscle in her entire body unless you counted her eyebrows, which she regularly flicked at the judges. They might've like it, but to me, she looked like Groucho Marx. Basically, she was one of these gals who would starve herself, survive on chicken broth and Cool Whip (that's right, Cool Whip—one calorie, zero carbohydrates—fake food) to look like an extra in a Van Halen video, then turn

The Good Girl Always Wins

into a fat cow addicted to Cool Ranch Doritos a week after the competition.

Okay, so I do my bit—dance, flex, pop, define. I am a virtual muscle magazine, baby. I ruled that stage. The whole Holiday Inn conference room stands up and applauds, wild-horse cheers. I see Kathy giving me the thumbs-up; Carol, another friend of mine from the gym, hollers, "Number one! Number one!"

Then Miss Cool Whip gets up there. The music starts, some George Michael song, "Why I Work So Hard for You," or some such hair-salon elevator-music thing. Cool Whip turns around and bends over. That's it. She bends over. All right, she has a repertoire of bend-over moves, but for the most part, she's looking back at the judges and shaking her ass while we're all laughing ours off.

The judges take less time to deliberate than a jury in Texas. I'm up there, standing next to Cool Whip. The guy who hands out the trophies grabs the heavyweight one and starts walking toward me while the announcer's reading, "And the winner of the heavyweight competition is . . ." You guessed it. Cool Whip. The trophy guy looks like he just took a spear to the shoulder blades, he's so stunned. Passes me, hands it to Cool Whip while everyone's booing, catcalling, swearing at the judges.

CHYNA

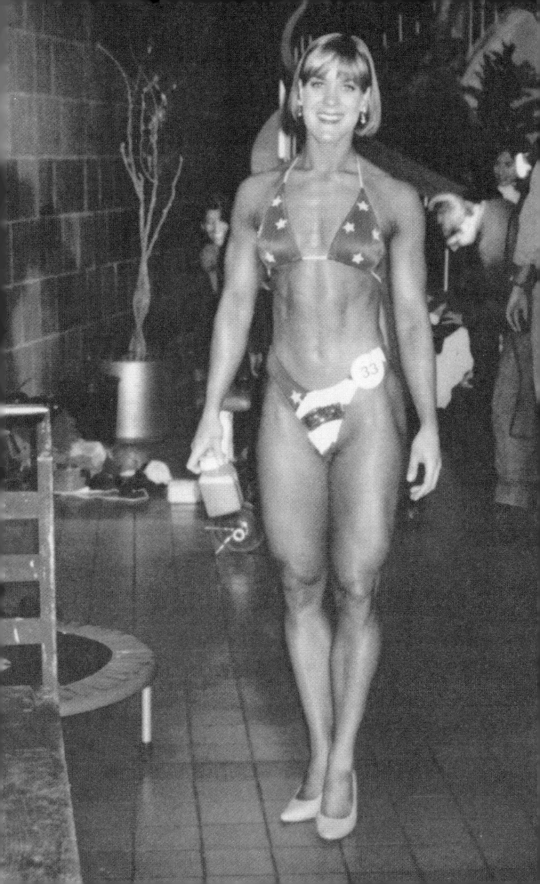

"YOU SUCK! YOU SUCK!" Suzy's yelling at Cool Whip, while my dad is trying to comfort me—"It was highway robbery, Muffin, everyone knows you outclassed the other girl"—while a big, noisy crowd forms around the judges, while I spot my friend, Carol, making her way toward the stage. The guy who passed the trophies out trails me out to the parking lot—I didn't know it until I'm turning in a circle yelling "FUCK SHIT RIP-OFFFFFFFF!!!!" at the top of my lungs and there he is.

"I'm so very sorry," he tells me. "I was so convinced that you won, I just started walking to you, and . . ." Well, it wasn't his fault, to be sure, but I still flipped him off because you know if you have Jan Laurer's blood coursing under your artificially darkened skin, everyone's part of a conspiracy.

I went up to my room to sulk. Opened the door and there, like an apparition, is the first-place trophy, sitting on the dresser. And there's Carol, slouched in my Holiday Inn occasional chair with a giant-ass shit-eating grin on her face.

"Congratulations, Joanie. You deserved it."

"Where did you get that?"

"Cool Whip thought the fix was in, too. She gave it to me to give to you."

"You're kidding me. She did?"

BAM! BAM! BAM! There's banging on the door. I can hear people out there, I can hear Cool Whip's little voice

CHINA *The Good Girl Always Wins*

squeaking in outrage, "She stole my trophy! She stole my trophy! She should be arrested!!" Carol looks at me, all that mischief turning to panic. She grabs the trophy, stuffs it under the mattress on the bed. I answer the door and the judges are there with Cool Whip hanging on one of them.

"I think you should consider giving back that trophy," this judge says, getting right to the point. "If you don't, you'll have to forfeit your NPC card." The National Physique Committee put together the competitions and you paid to be a member. I could feel my jaw muscles tightening.

"Take a fucking hike. We don't have your piece-of-shit trophy," Carol's hollering over my shoulder. "You wanna find it, maybe you should look up her ass!!!!"

"Carol, Carol." I'm trying to calm her down and deal with these assholes at the same time.

"Are you serious? You're gonna take away my NPC card because you picked the wrong winner?"

The lead judge gestures for his posse to move along, then gives me one last verbal shot in the chops.

"You bodybuilders look in the mirror and think you all look so great." Ouch. Now in another time, i.e., today, I would've, one, screamed in his face, "YOU'RE DAMN RIGHT!!!"; two, kicked his ass; or three, stuffed the trophy up his ass. But after they left we just threw the trophy in the garbage. The nonconfrontational Joanie tried to for-

CHYNA

get about the whole pathetic mess. But long after the hand-print on my back faded away, the stain of the (skeleton) Key West Body-Building Contest stayed with me.

And so I am here, in front of the ESPN2 cameras, I am here as a gesture of defiance, knowing I'll be ridiculed, knowing people will talk into their petite little hands about me, but knowing that in another place, a very big place, full of color and spectacle and excitement, that I am an object of, of, of . . . of DESIRE! True, the WWF hadn't called yet, but it was only a matter of time. So let's just see how Joanie Laurer competes when she's got the horsepower, when she's got a little self-confidence under her belt, shall we, girlie-girls?

"From Lowell, Massachusetts, JOANIE LIAR!"

Three previous competitions and the mo-fos still couldn't pronounce my name. I step forward in my belly-dancing costume and the crowd starts buzzing—it's not a cheer, more like the noise in a really crowded restaurant. Nobody quite knows what to expect. My music cues up—belly-dancing music—and now these clowns are leaning forward on their seats. I put everything on the line, all the sweet, provocative moves of the undulating stomach, the snaking hips, the enticing arms, all so expertly taught to me by the eighty-year-old genius chanteuse, Zebeida. There's shouting, whistling as I do a coy pirouette, give them a taste of the Laurer tush, the Coolio Culo, the baby got back. By the time I make the full revolution, the crowd is clapping, frothing in delight! And then I drop my sword on my foot. There is this collective moan from the nearly three thousand people in the audience, "OOOOOOOHHHHHH," that can probably be heard in Istanbul. And I know what you're thinking—I blew it. Last place. You wanna know what? I dropped the sword on purpose. And you know why? Because I wanted last place. Granted, I probably would've gotten last place anyway, but why leave anything to chance? I wanted last place because I wanted the roses. And last place made what I was about to do all the more satisfying.

At the end of the Fitness America Pageant, everyone who competes gets a dozen roses and there's this photo shoot backstage—all for the sake of good sportsmanship. "And, although she finished last, let's give a hand to Joanie Laurer." The steward hands me my dozen roses. I take a big whiff, then fling them to the floor and march proudly for the door, crying.

"Hey, come back here." One of the pageant organizers is trailing me. "We don't end things in this way here, we want everybody to hug."

"Fuck off!" I roared. And I never felt more like a winner in my entire life. That was my last Fitness America Pageant.

CHYNA

January 1997 I am on the toilet, doing my toe-nails, applying polish to each toe, and I am talking to each toe, telling it a little story: This little piggy got fired from MobileCom. This little piggy made exactly thirty-nine dollars over the past two months because this little piggy's unemployment benefits just ran out. This little piggy finished dead last in the Fitness America Pageant, and this time they will find a way to never let you come back. This little piggy broke up with a boyfriend who just might be the kindest, most understanding, and decent man in America. (His name is Jerry, he's a trainer; loved him to death but not nearly as much as he loved me. I think he called me his "Power Bar" once and that was the beginning of the end, as far as I was concerned.) And this little piggy, who thinks she's going to be a big pro-wrestling star, can't even find a woman her size to fight and had to beat some guy with fake tits and a mask. Hmmm . . . I'm thinking of skipping my other foot when the phone rings.

"Hey, how you doin'? Listen, I'm in town, thought maybe you'd wanna possibly work out. You *do* work out?"

"Of course, I do. By the way, who is this?"

"Hunter."

Oh, Jesus.

I drive to the gym, thinking, is this really a workout we're about to have or is this, wink, wink, a workout we're

CHYNA

about to have? Calm down, Joanie, calm down, be your-self—check that—be some of yourself, but most of all, take everything at face value. See, that was my new approach to life. In the immortal words of the great philosopher, Nike, *just do it.* Joanie, don't overthink it. Let it happen, girl, and for God's sake stop looking for ulterior motives. The old man again. I have Joe the L to thank for that little hang-up. When you're raised by Joe Laurer, when your role model hires bodyguards in Colombia for inexplicable reasons, you tend to question the intentions of others more than usual. "But, Dad, we don't know the first thing about the sport of curling," I remember saying when he was planning to join that ultraexclusive club in the Northeast. "Sure, we do, Muffin," he replied. "The first thing to know is that most of those people have a lot of money."

"Okay, thanks for coming," Hunter says to me at the gym. "Where do you want to start?"

"It's your call, whatever you want."

"Okay, let's do chest."

"Excuse me?"

"Chest. Bench press?"

"Oh, right, sure, sure." I nod.

"I, uh, like to go heavy duty, forced reps to failure. You okay with that?" he asks me. Now, I swear on the lives of my unborn grandchildren that this is exactly how I like to

The Good Girl Always Wins

train. Go all-out, gonzo hard for a short period, cool down, then repeat it. So, right off, Hunter and I have something in common. When we start lifting, however, we both painfully discover a major difference, and besides the time I grabbed his ankles (which I'll get to later on), this is one of Hunter's favorite Hunter/Chyna stories. So I'll let him take it from here. Hunter?

Hi, everyone, what's up? First of all, that line about "Let's do chest?" I meant it totally innocently. I meant, you know, let's work on each other's — I mean, *our* chest muscles. The pecs and like that. All right: We're in the gym and Joanie and I are ready to start. I begin by putting 135 pounds on the bar, do a few reps — repetitions — to warm up. Joanie puts 135 pounds up, does the same thing, and right off, I'm thinking, Wow. Most women *top off* at 135 pounds. When she's done with her set of 135, Joanie grabs another ninety, throws it on. She's at 225 now. I'm thinking, Jesus Christ, she's gonna do that? Uh-huh, sure, she's trying to get a job, trying to impress me. She'll do a few reps and peter out. We both do the 225. And she just smacks it out, ten reps, just like that, no strain. Before I can catch my breath,

CHYNA

she cranks it up to *315*. Now, I'm thinking, No fucking way! This is gonna cut her in half. But she grabs it, boom, boom, two reps. No sweat, like she's pumping sponge cake here.

In my head? I'm thinking, God, I haven't gone up to 315 *myself*. I hope I can even hit that! And at the time, I clocked in at 230 on the scales, probably outweigh her by fifty pounds. So I don't want to be shown up here. I'm gonna try for a triple — three lifts. On the third one I blew one of my nuts halfway across the room. I am, like, wasted. She? She wants to do frigging *leg presses*. She throws every plate she can fit on the machine — you're talking, like, fifteen hundred pounds, two thousand pounds on a leg press. When it's my turn, I make some crybaby excuse about hurting my knees in a match recently because I flat-out couldn't do what she was doing.

Look, she pushed me and that was a great thing. Hey, I knew she wanted to get hired, but this girl had a work ethic like you wouldn't believe. That time up in the motel room? She had business cards, she had photos, she had the portfolio, she had résumés, she had videotapes edited to music. Everybody says she was lucky. Well, I

CHYNA

don't believe that. You make your own luck. Hard
work puts you in a position to be in the right place
at the right time. And that's what Joanie did.
Walter's school? All the dudes over there who
complained, "I've been here longer than she was,
I should've gotten a shot way before she did."
Those are the ones who sit back waiting for someone to walk in and say, "Hey, would you like to be
world champion of the WWF?" Well, not Joanie.
Joanie had the courage, she had the nerve, she had
the guts . . .

Oh, hi, there. I guess I let him go on a little too long, heh,
heh. Hunter. Nice man, isn't he? Sometimes I feel so much
sympathy for him, other times I think he thinks he's got me
fooled, other times I think he's really got me fooled, and
then there's those times where if I could prove that I was
right about what I think he's thinking, I'd have his legs broken. Men lead such confusing lives.

Hunter and I continued our workouts together whenever he was in town and we kept the relationship at that
level. I'm not going to say that I wasn't attracted to him,
because I was, I liked him and vice versa. But this job that I
wanted was the most important thing in the world to me,
and I think we both wanted it to work professionally for us.

CHYNA

The Good Girl Always Wins

So what happens? The twelve labors of Hercules, that's what. Hunter comes to Lowell. And brings the entire WWF with him. The bookers scheduled a house show in Lowell, but you get the picture. It seemed like the worst possible coincidence.

"So, you're coming, right? I left you a pass," Hunter said on the phone.

"I don't think so. I have other plans."

"Oh, yeah, right. Come on, Joanie, you should be there, hanging out."

"Now, how's that gonna look, Hunter? Everyone knows I want a job. I'll look like just another rat." Rats were groupies. And, really, I had tried everything to get hired. I'd been to other shows, and I wasn't about to go and stand there and look like a rejected idiot.

The night the WWF came to town I went out to dinner with a friend to forget. Hunter called up a half-hour before the show. "Are you sure, are you sure? You don't want to go?" Not when I can have lumpy, overcooked fettuccine served by a waiter with filthy fingernails and a fake Ice-T lisp.

I got home around eight o'clock, figured I'd get some much-unneeded rest, maybe watch the rest of *Requiem for a Heavyweight*. Anthony Quinn, contender for the heavy-weight title, suffers an eye injury that ends his boxing career. Gotta eat, right? So his agent gets him this really humiliating job as a pro wrestler. They give him a hatchet, a war bonnet, and this Indian blanket and bill him as The Big Chief. I'm crying my eyes out when the phone rings; it's Hunter and he's breathless.

"Joanie. It's a go!"

"A go. What's a go?"

"Vince just hired you!"

"WHAT!!!????"

"Yeah! Get down to the building right now! Hurry up!"

"Say again, Hunter."

"Joooaniiiee . . ."

"Please? You hardly know me, right? RIGHT? But you gotta know what this means to me. Now, please—"

"Joan. You're hired."

YEAAAAAAAAAAAAAAAHHHHHHHHHHHHH-HHHHH!

CHINA *The Good Girl Always Wins*

10

All You Need Is a Good Gimmick

Diane Keaton should know better.

She's a smart gal, good actress, so-so director, but more important, has an impressive list of ex-boyfriends. So she should
definitely know better. We appeared on Leno together and
whenever her eyes met mine she had this look on her face that
said it all. She flashed that look people get when they see
Casey and Jean Casem together, that look Nancy Kerrigan
gave to Tonya Harding when they sat down to reconcile, that
look everybody had for Ben Stiller when he hosted the MTV
Music Awards. She was pompous and condescending, and for
someone who hasn't changed her image since 1958 or something, for someone who relies on the Frida Kahlo look, but-
toned up to the neck and skittish as a circus pony, she should
know better. She should know that when she's looking at me in
my shrink-wrap leather Batman outfit and six-inch stiletto
heels, bloodred lipstick and eighteen-inch biceps, she's looking at herself, okay? We all have our crutches, our devices, our
ploys, our signatures. So don't be glaring at me like I've got a
finger crammed up my nostril, all right? We all have our little
ways of surviving, of being heard, okay? And some of us don't
even deserve the opportunity! Look at this phony, Goldberg,
over in the WCW. He doesn't even know how to wrestle,
Diane! He's Uncle Fester with a scowl! He comes in, they let
him win every single match that he ever did, and presto, he's
a star? I don't think so. He does an interview and he's the real

CHYNA

deal, you know, like all the rest of us are fake, but not Goldberg, no way. Those guys over there like him, they get a hangnail and they don't wrestle for months! They work when they feel like it, Diane! They don't care! They're lazy and, and, and . . . where was I? Oh, yeah—I'm hired!! I'm hired!!

Of course, Vince McMahon had his own special way of doing business, which meant bloodshed. Nobody gets anything for free. Like I said, the real artistes among us? The true aficionados of the sport? We don't care about who wins and who loses. And thank God, Hunter is an artiste, because he's the one who took it on the chin. Take it, Hunter:

Hey. The night Joanie got the word, right? It's a winter night, and we're in Lowell for a special *Thursday Night Raw*. That night, the big match involved Seanie, Sean Michaels, losing the WWF championship belt. It was sad, because Sean was so beat up, he had to give up the belt. His knee was a complete mess, his back all out of whack. When it was over, Sean comes up to me, says, "Tonight I lost the belt and my smile, Hunter." He basically went out there and gave up the world title because he couldn't physically wrestle anymore. I was the intercontinental champ at the time and they came to me and asked me—*Vince*

All You Need Is a Good Gimmick

came to me and asked me to do this little favor.
They needed something exciting in the beginning
of the new show — that would be when we first
went to two shows a week, the second being
SmackDown! Vince wanted to know if I would
work with this new guy named Rocky Maivia, who
is now, of course, The Rock. Vince wanted me to
drop the intercontinental belt to him that night
on TV. But when he asked me to do it he really was
smart, setting me up by saying, almost like an
afterthought, "Oh, and by the way, I've decided to
give it a try with that girl you want to bring in.
But she's your responsibility. And you bring her
along slowly." So that's Vince for you. I get what I
always wanted. And so does he. And more.

So I get in the car and drive through a half-dozen red lights
to get to the Lowell arena before the show's over. Oh, I have
wings, dear friends, I am the FTD guy in a Metallica video.
No one was gonna stop me now. You wanna stop me, huh?
I'm looking at myself in the rearview mirror. Then you better bring tools, bring a lunch, bring enough rations for a
nuclear holocaust, because, baby, it's gonna take that long!

When I get there, I have to do something to get my
heart to quiet down. Breathe, Joanie, breathe. I am told that

CHYNA

I actually met Vince McMahon, but I swear I have no recollection of it—that's how overwhelmed I was. Remember Hunter, telling you how Vince told him to bring me along slowly? The next day I was in Germany to begin a seventeen-day European tour.

■ ■ ■

At its best, coming into WWF pro wrestling as a beginner is like suddenly having a private table at the best restaurant in town. You have arrived, girl, and millions of people are gonna be shouting your name. Your scowling breasts will stare out at kids from the posters of you that they've pinned to their closet doors. It's movin' on up to the East Side, to a deluxe apartment in the sky, it's a dream come true in a dream come true. But at its worst, it's a combination of walking the prison yard for the first time and *Showgirls*. Guys on the circuit come and go regularly; faces change. New stars are built up, old ones limp off. Others are built up but just don't click with the audiences and end up as security guards, nightclub bouncers, or worse. You come in new, everybody's checking you out. You come in new as a woman, they are checking you over. And if you come in as a woman who looks like she could break Xena in half, it's *over and out*. You get everything from being called a dyke to getting propositioned for a threesome. On that European tour? I got worked, I got hazed, I got the initiation of a lifetime. And that was just the fans. Vince and the WWF

All You Need Is a Good Gimmick

brought me in as a heel, a bad guy. It began with me sitting in the crowd like any ordinary, attractive female spectator. Hunter would have his match (at the time, his character was kind of a cheater, a coward, a jerk—or what Shane McMahon's character is today), and I, the Mystery Woman, would bolt out of my seat and rescue Hunter, kick his opponent's ass, blindside the dude, yank his legs out from under him, nail him in the nuts when he wasn't looking. The fans immediately loved to hate me, which was good. They threw batteries at me, spit in my face, power-flung beer into my chest, called me a cunt, chick-with-dick, dyke—which was bad. And like I said, that was just the fans. And the guys? To their credit, nobody hung a dead cat in my locker or slipped a roofie in my Gatorade, but it's safe to say I think you know when you go somewhere and you're not wanted. You get earplay: "This is a man's world." "You don't belong here." "You're not hitting me, and if you do I'm not gonna register it, and you're gonna look like an idiot." "Stay out of the locker room—stay out of our business." "I wasn't talking to you."

Here, let me briefly hand it over to one of the sweetest human beings on the face of the planet, Mick Foley:

Do I remember the first time I met Chyna? Hell, yeah. I thought she was really full of herself and I didn't like her at all. I thought she came off as a

CHYNA

prima donna. She'd come around, like, "Hello, everybody, I wish I could stop and talk but I really can't." First time I actually saw her wrestle she was shaking Terry Reynolds around and my first thought was, My God, what kind of woman is this? Later on, around February of '97, I think it was, I saw her wrestle again. My wife came to the event and when my wife congratulated her on the great job she had done, Joanie was so grateful, just being very appreciative of the compliment. And that was the first time I really got a sense of who she was. At that point, she was wrestling as the psychotic fan who's later revealed to be in cahoots with Triple H. It wasn't until two years ago that she really started wrestling regularly. Up until then it was her job to get involved in the matches, put her two cents in. And her two cents were usually painful ones. And it's true — some of the guys were hesitant to have her involved in a match. A certain some-one — I won't name names — put it

CHYNA

eloquently: "Ain't gonna let no bitch hit me." My feeling was, well, why not? She's stronger than most of the guys. I was very open to the idea of her hitting me and causing me physical harm during the matches. We'd go out of our way to let something big happen and let her look impressive. For her to body-slam me at three hundred pounds is impressive, and I don't mind. I've had guys less formidable, so why not her? She hits a lot harder than most of the guys, which in some ways is not fair because I still feel funny about hitting Chyna. I don't know what it is. I only had one real match with her—I was holding back and she wasn't. She was making real good contact with my cranium. You know what else? I used to joke about the sexual tension between my character, Mankind, and Chyna and point to her revealing outfits and me wearing mine where I'm covered almost from head to toe. The basis for my feeling was that her hand would contact with my genitals several times—

Uh, Mick—

—it didn't matter if the hand was balled up in a fist or traveling at high speeds—

CHYNA

Mick—

**—technically, there was still contact being made.
Mankind saw that as a sexual thing.**

Well, I think you get the picture. I love Mick, and it wasn't just
the wrestling. I had to travel with these guys, be on the road
with them 250 days out of the year. I had to dress with them,
eat with them, joke, cry, laugh, live with them, and try to make
myself part of what was heretofore a man's world. Yeah, sure, I
had Hunter and Sean Michaels in my corner and they were, as
we say in wrestling, in the spot. They were hot, they were big,
they had enough star power to use me in the correct way, to get
me a shot at a higher level, to skip a few rungs. If I had come in
at a lower level . . . well, you know what? They don't let you in
at a lower level, so it never would've happened anyway. And
also, Hunter and I became romantically involved. First thing
we had to do was hide it—at least, that's how he felt about it. I
wanted to be recognized for my talent, not who I was sharing a
bed with. I wanted to be respected as a wrestler, as a performer
on a par with the men, not as some Bend-Over Betty who
sucked and fucked her way to the top. Not like Cool Whip,
who stole that trophy by shaking her ass. So I had to walk the
walk, gain the guys' respect inch by inch. Yet I was confused.
Why did I have to go and fall in love with him? Yeah, I wanted

All You Need Is a Good Gimmick

the guys' respect, but I also wanted Hunter's. Respect is such a big issue for me. I didn't want the relationship with the man of my dreams to be behind closed doors. It was just another feeling of rejection to me, of me. It was a feeling of Hunter being embarrassed to be with me. I used to feel so hurt when Hunter's regular "rats" would show up at the airports, the buildings, the gyms. He would make up some excuse as to why they couldn't suck his dick that night, they would hug, and we would be on our way; platonic Hunter and his bodyguard. I would get pissed off and Hunter would argue, "But Buffy was a nice girl. Why should I be mean to her?" or "Susie always

picks me up in Baltimore. I don't want you to be upset when you see her!"

Upset? Oh, no, why would I be upset, Paul? I'm having a relationship with a man who won't acknowledge me in public. But the respectable dick-suckers can get hugs and smiles or a great breakfast with me sitting at the table getting sick to my stomach.

Now in Hunter's defense, before me he was a single, awesome-looking guy with new fame, new money, and a body to die for. There were women all over him and as they say, "when in Rome, do as the Romans do," so that's just what he did. However, after we got more involved, the groupies faded, the rats scuttled away, and Hunter lost some of his cheese! (Thank God.) The truth is, he didn't even give a shit about any of them. Paul was in love with me. But he just couldn't acknowledge that, because he was more concerned about his job, his position, what people might say. Okay, let me get this straight. The same people who probably couldn't care less about what he did personally? The same people who are dying to get some great gossip on one of us? The same people who were screwing different broads every night of the week while their wives and kids were home sleeping? Are those the same people that would give us a hard time if they knew we were together? Hmm. . . . Now I'm not saying that everyone partakes in this behavior, but it is certainly considered acceptable.

All You Need Is a Good Gimmick

Okay, so I went with it at first and kept my mouth shut. Then, after a while, I didn't give a fuck who found out. Believe me, I had been paying my dues. I was working hard and performing well. The fact is, we just felt differently about the situation. I didn't like it, but I loved Paul. I just think Hunter looked at it from a complete "business" point of view. This really makes sense, because in reality Hunter treats this business like the perfect wife. He loves it, he works hard at the relationship, he thinks about it all the time, he nurtures it, he protects it, he embraces it wholly. He couldn't live without it; he makes it his number one priority. Point being Triple H really did marry Stephanie McMahon, or her company, anyway, and I was his mistress. I mean, some things you can't change—ever.

For example, there are bad wrestlers, plain and simple. Bad moves, slow, unconvincing, uncompelling performers— regardless of how much they accept and like you, they're just bad. Consequently, wrestling them makes you look bad—or gets you hurt. There are people I wrestle that I am comfortable with, that I know will protect me. Then there are those who are careless. Those who wrestle with the careless end up with their teeth kicked in or a black eye. Some call it "working stiff." Then there are the kooks. Cactus Jack was a crazy hardcore kook. Look at all that stuff he did to his body: explosions, thumbtacks, falling off steel cages, and let's not forget the painful "butt punch"! I mean, that's not normal! Also, Mick is one of the only ones who really

likes my sense of humor, and that's not normal, either! Jericho is also a kook. A fun kook. He's got that rock star/warrior/blowhard thing working overtime. And that signature double-take—puh-leeze. A better double-take is the one that Kane gets when you see him for the first time. He's got the best body of them all. His body says "Don't fuck with me" in a big, cornfed way, and I think that's cool. Billy G. has that whole *GQ* look down. I think we would make a great-looking television couple one day. Billy and I know all the words to "Purple Rain." Then there's Hunter, possibly the best and hardest worker in the business today. Knows his shit, man, and knows it good. Undertaker, respected by all. Dogg and X-Pac—say one word about me and "your ass is grass. . . ." I love the guys, and the guys who, in the beginning, were meanest to me, hated me the most, and didn't want me to be there, now give me my daily dosages of affection and are my biggest supporters. Steve Austin was the first person who acted like a steam-roller hit him when I decked him. (Who's cooler than Stone Cold?) And the boys saw me fuck up early on. I mean in my little climb to the top, I fell on my face a time or two.

Joanie Screw-up #1, December 1998, Pay-Per-View I am the bad girl, a big enough heel to use on a shoe made for Godzilla. Hunter's in the ring, and it's a cage match against your friend and mine, Mankind. I was never a huge fan of cage matches. Visually,

CHYNA

they look great. Like put a couple of gorillas in a phone booth and see who ends up top banana. Thing is, what are the two wrestlers gonna do? Kill each other? Go to sleep? Kiss and make up? Or beat each other senseless? Maybe they can just chase each other in a circle until they both turn into butter. I don't know, it is supposed to add all this drama, but to me, all it does is limit the performers. I am thinking about all of this, by the way, as I lie prone, outside the caged ring, after Mankind flipped me into (pretend) unconsciousness. Now, because I can't see anything, we arranged a signal beforehand. I would hear a particular sound—which would be Hunter slammed to the mat by Mankind—and that would be my cue to stir and drag him to safety. Somewhere along the line I lost track of time . . .

Kaboooom! I hear it, grope for Hunter's legs. Got 'em! Start to pull—

"WHAT THE HELL ARE YOU DOING?" Hunter's whispering to me as I drag him by the ankles, "WHAT ARE YOU, NUTS??? PUT ME BACK!!!" I can barley hear him over the crowd, but I can tell something's really, really wrong. Because Mankind is lying flat on the mat, dazed and confused. The sound I heard was Mankind getting body-slammed by Hunter. "IT'S NOT TIME YET! IT'S NOT TIME YET! ACT LIKE YOU'RE CHECKING ON ME AND GET OUT!"

"WHAT?" I'm frantic, I can't hear a thing he's saying until

All You Need Is a Good Gimmick

it hits me—Oh yeah! Of course! So I check on Hunter, give him my best *General Hospital* look of concern, and slink away from Hunter and Mankind faster than you can say Chef Boyardee.

Naturally, I was crushed, felt horrible, but Hunter was forgiving.

"Look," he told me after the match, "X-Pac? He's my best friend, right? Great performer, rarely screws up, but when he does he blows a gasket, no matter how small it is. You want some advice?"

"I want a back rub."

"We'll get to that. You want advice? Unless you have a blatant screw-up that messes everything up, that has people booing and pissing and laughing, that has Vince blowing a nut, you just forget about it. You go on to the next thing. You think on your feet." Not like that time Val and I went through the Spanish announcers' table and ruined Hunter and Rock's big finish. I remember Hunter screaming in the hallway, "Fuck! Motherfucker! They what?"

Well, you get the picture. Val and I felt horrible.

Chyna Screw-up #2, February 1999

(Note: If you haven't noticed already, I refer to myself as Joanie in screw-up #1 and refer to myself as Chyna in this one. That's because by this time, I was beginning to actually

feel comfortable being called Chyna. For a while there, someone would say, "Hey, Chyna," and I'd react like a brood mare with brain damage—first you see the lightning, then you hear the thunder. For a while, I wasn't seeing the lightning. By the way, about the name "Chyna": The WWF was in Las Vegas one weekend when Vince decided that the Mystery Woman needed to be introduced. And that, really, was a big moment for me, my christening. What's in a name?

Everything and nothing. Would the Beatles have been as big as they were if they'd been called the Bugs? Would *Jaws* have had the same impact had it been called *The Shark*? Who can say? All I know is the name list compiled by the WWF creative department included Teeva Gweeve, Phalan, Sheera, Venus, and Tigress. Teeva Gweeve? What is that all about? Sounds like the name of a female pig in a cartoon. Phalan? Sheera? Right. Why didn't they just come out and call me Butch Woman? As it turned out, Vince liked Chyna, the play on words. If you think of Chyna, you think of fine china, something fragile, something delicate, and he got off on the idea that here was this muscular, brutal woman who was beating the hell out of all these guys. Beats the hell out of Teeva Gweeve, that's all I can say.)

On to screw-up #2: Tonight, the mighty Kane will shoot a fireball into my face. He'll be aiming for Hunter, but Hunter ducks and I get it flush in the kisser. The whole thing sounds good on paper.

"It looks like a napkin almost and it's highly combustible." Steve, the prop man, is explaining to me, Hunter, and Kane how the weapon will work. "Kane here's gonna aim and pull the trigger. The trigger is actually a flint that will spark, set the napkin on fire, then propel the napkin at you. By the time the napkin—which will look like a ball of fire—by the time it reaches you it'll be out. It's like fire-

CHYNA

works. By the time the cinders hit the ground, they're out. But it'll look like you've been hit. You wanna practice it a few times?"

We did and it worked perfectly every time. But I could feel a tiny burst of heat near my face for a split second, as if your hairdresser got distracted with the blow dryer aimed at your face. It made me a little apprehensive.

"I don't know about this, guys"—I started to say, but judging by their looks (I was a poor judge; I was wrong, as it turned out), I sensed (incorrectly) that the p-word (pussy) was taking shape in the hinterlands of their realm of all things macho so I thought on my feet, made them think I was talking about something else—"you think I should wear my hair off my face, or not?"

By the time our, er, *match* came up, I was no longer concerned. One big reason was because we were in Pittsburgh, and Eugene was in the house. Eugene is in his early twenties and developmentally handicapped. He's one of my biggest fans and every time we play Pittsburgh, he's there, yelling his head off for me as one of the ring boys.

All right. We have the match. Everyone's lovin' it, me conspiring all of a sudden with Kane. I put the big-ass body lock on Hunter, squeeze him like an orange. Kane brandishes the flame thrower, pulls the trigger, and suddenly everything goes slow-mo. I can see the wad of paper hurl-

CHYNA

ing toward my face and it's smoking, changing into something alive, then POOOF! The thing ignites in a flash. Ever been spattered by bacon grease? It felt kind of like that, only if somebody threw the whole pan at you. I went down. When I first felt it, I thought there'd be a real good chance that in the future I'd be wrestling in a mask just like Kane. I was blinded in one eye for about two days and the fire singed off my eyelashes on one eye. I was okay, but Eugene—remember Eugene?—was hysterically crying. It was killing him. After they patched me up, put gauze on my eye, I went out and comforted Eugene, assuring him I was okay. Kane felt terrible, too, blamed himself, but it was a total freak thing for the ball to ignite as late as it did, and if you tried to do it again, it might not happen that way in a million years. My sight came back, but my eyelashes didn't fare as well. Grew in halfway. And down instead of up. From that day on, I became the Tammy Faye Bakker of the WWF. Had to wear fake eyelashes. Amen.

11

Nobody Holds a Grudge

I have a good match tonight, lotta action, lotta fun. Eddie and I go after Chris Benoit and Shane and totally kick their asses. I get to do my flippy thing—the ninja somersault move that might one day get me a Dramamine endorsement. Lawler's still thinking of a name to call it: the Chyna Spring Roll, Jumping Jack Flash, the, er, Pin Wheel, but until he comes up with something that doesn't make me gag, I'm sticking with the Flippy. Besides, the idea that Jerry "The King" Lawler, a sweetheart of a guy but about as macho as a chain saw, has to say the word "flippy" during *Raw Is War* just makes me kind of smile inside. The match is booked for me to lose on a technicality, which is kind of a bummer, but it's all part of the deal, especially if I'm battling against the guys. You're part of a story line. So many of us forget that part, so many of us hate to lose. Being a woman might help a little. I mean, we're used to getting dumped on, right? But the guys, they take it hard. I remember walking past Vince Russo's office one time when Russo, one of the top writers in pro wrestling, was still with the WWF. He had a wrestler in there with him, a guy I happen to be quite fond of actually, but this guy was going on and on, singeing Vince Russo's eyebrows.

"I beat this guy, I beat this guy, and now I have to lose? Look at my record—"

"Wait a minute, wait a minute." Russo cut him off. "*You*

CHYNA

didn't beat anybody, okay? We wrote stories that had you winning, remember? Your win-loss record? That's fiction, that's Superman getting sick around Kryptonite, okay? It ain't the real deal, my friend!"

Or take Mick Foley—now the commissioner! In his book, *Have a Nice Day*, he talks about his matches, what went wrong, what went right. He wrote about how he won the championship belt, something wrestlers want to do all their lives, wrote about it almost as if it was real. But let me tell you what was real: Mick wrote that book, longhand, in spiral notebooks, worked on it in the middle of the night, after matches, after doing things to his body that no stuntman in a Schwarzenegger movie could ever come close to doing. He wrote it dead tired, drained, and aching, on airplanes flying between performances. While the rest of us were snoring in coach, our backs and legs cramping up, he's corked into his own teeny little coach seat with the little light on and he's scribbling away. That's the part that's real. That's the part that's not predetermined. The fire, the passion, the determination? The wrestling writers can't manufacture that for you. As good as he is, Vince McMahon can't reach into his bag of gimmicks and provide that for you. That part— the most important part—comes from within. The crowd doesn't respond to you because of your impressive record, they respond to you because you entertain them. And when

Nobody Holds a Grudge

I finally won the intercontinental title? I am proud to say that people talked about that match for months—not just because a woman beat a man, not just because it truly was a chaotic, hysterical, and very intense romp over the mat, but because we pulled it off. Just barely.

Intercontinental title. Now, what exactly does that mean, when you break it down? See, here again lies the genius of Vince McMahon. Intercontinental. It sounds grand, important, and completely bogus all at once. It sounds full of shit—and I mean that entirely as a compliment. It sounds like the kind of term some college kid would use to try to fake his way through an interview for a paralegal position or the name of a really classy gentlemen's club. Anyway, Jeff Jarrett held the title, and, as it turned out, the whole WWF by the balls. My big chance? Chyna, Ninth Wonder of the World, first woman to defeat a man in a title match? Almost didn't happen.

Two things nearly shot the whole match to pieces. First of all, it was called the Good Housekeeping match, right? Well, bad record keeping almost ruined it—seems there was this little oversight that somehow got past the WWF

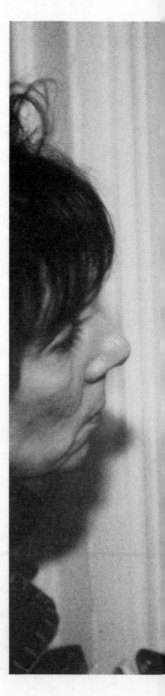

brain trust, which in itself is an intercontinental feat. Believe me, nothing gets past these people. Normally, you couldn't pass a fart between Vince McMahon and his legal department, they were that tight. But the real problem was success. The whole deal between Jarrett and myself just worked too well.

Some months before our match, word around the big black tower in Stamford was that Vince McMahon was going through a major case of buyer's remorse. He shelled out megabank to sign Jarrett to his last contract, and over the past year, Jarrett's popularity was on the downswing. And this despite the fact that the WWF promoted the hell out of him, changed his name, his outfit, and even his hairstyle. Probably the best example of wretched excess was during Jarrett's Electric Horseman phase.

One night, we're all backstage—I think it was in Buffalo—limbering up, getting ready for our matches. I look over at Kane and he's got his nose in the air, pulls off his mask.

CHYNA

"What the fuck is that smell?" He's frowning. Now we're all smelling it.

"Horseshit," Hunter snaps.

"No, I really smell something bad," Kane counters. He looks a little hurt.

"I smell it too, Paul," I insist.

"Horseshit. It's *horse* shit. There, you see?" Paul points down the cement corridor. There is Jeff Jarrett, on a real live horse and in this cowboy getup, neon lights outlining his physique, making him glow like Robert Redford in *The Electric Horseman.* Which actually looked pretty damn cool—until you realized the horse he was riding was actually a pony. And this one might've been part Shetland. Because Jeff's feet touched the ground. Eventually, they got a horse that fit him, but the whole thing just didn't go over. As I've said before, if there's one thing you can tell, it's when the crowd isn't with something, when they just ain't buyin' it. And in this case they were saying, er, "Nay."

"Fuck the horse. Put him with Chyna," McMahon ordered Vince Russo one morning before Russo did his customary thing, which was to go off and write from his home.

"Chyna. And Jarrett. Like . . . ?"

"Book a PPV title match and let 'em kick the shit out of each other." McMahon, I am told, sort of laughed to himself, and shook his head. When he does this it usually means he's

CHYNA

at his wit's end. Last-straw time. Russo had been champing at the bit for a while to get me up against a guy in a title match—I mean, I'd like to think we were all heading in that direction—but he wasn't sure Jarrett was the right choice.

"He's got a problem with heat right now, Vince," Russo countered. "If we're gonna do this, shouldn't we go with someone bigger?"

"Book 'em. We're not gonna re-sign him anyway. It solves a ton of problems. And, besides . . ." Vince trailed off, didn't finish the sentence.

Russo then did a very smart thing—he asked for time to manufacture a little rivalry between us, a little buildup to work it.

There were a handful of rumors floating around as to why Vince ultimately paired me up with Jeff. Some people saw it as a natural—Jeff being six feet even, with his build (he had great muscle tone but didn't look like a Lego toy), the blond hair against my black wig would look good in the ring, square dancing into a clothesline with me—it was kind of sexy. But in the end, the way the whole thing played out? Maybe it wasn't up there with who shot JFK, but you just had to think conspiracy. Most of the guys bought the Magic Bullet Proposition, a two-for-one deal: I was on the way up and pairing me with him would help put Jarrett, a big investment, over. But looking back on it (twenty-twenty hind-

sight, yeah, yeah), I'd have to go with the Two Gunmen Theory. Back when Vince McMahon suggested the pairing, he probably had no intention of re-signing Jeff Jarrett; Vince was ready to cut bait, eat his investment. Pairing us — Chyna, the woman, Jarrett, the man — was a gamble Vince couldn't lose. Do it on Pay-Per-View. If it goes over, everyone loves it, Vince keeps me up there, pairing me with the guys, working in a title match here and there. Sure, a rematch with Jarrett is out of the question since he'll be gone, but nothing was working with him *anyway*. If the whole lovely intergender bite-me fest doesn't come off, well, Jarrett's gone and Vince doesn't have to worry about a rematch. Not only that, but Jarrett, a money pit for the WWF so far, goes out as a loser. (You think they were gonna let him *win*? He was leaving.)

Here's where it gets a little far-fetched, I admit it, but those late-night drives from city to city do crazy things to your head. Lotta time to think, know what I'm saying? In a freaky way, the real and the imagined smack into each other out on the highway, late at night. And

CHYNA · *Nobody Holds a Grudge*

here, here at this juncture in my wrestling career—this whole business about competing with a man, about making it look convincing—the phony and the actual were colliding again. Remember what Vince said when Hunter and Sean went to him about me? "What's she gonna do, beat up all the guys? They're not gonna go for it." While Vince came around, got on board, and eventually welcomed the Chyna character into the fold, he still knew a little bit about human nature. Is there a chance that he might've got some satisfaction out of knowing Jeff Jarrett was leaving the WWF as the first man to lose to a woman? Nah, after all, I didn't *really* beat him . . . right?

Vince Russo wrote bits between Jeff and myself leading up to the big title match, stuff where Jeff would run out, blindside me during a match with a toaster, then run away.

"Chyna, are you gonna run and hide like every other woman would and should do? 'Cause there ain't a chance in hell you're gonna beat me!" Jarrett would holler from

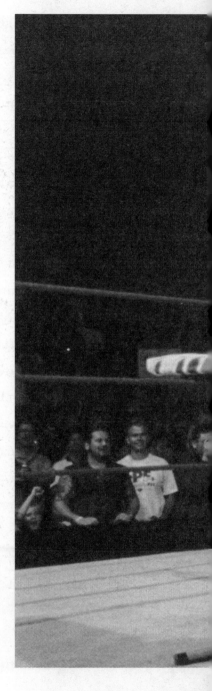

CHYNA

the ring after winning a match. Then he'd bolt out into the audience and humiliate some poor, defenseless woman (on the WWF payroll), make her vacuum up some dirt he threw in the aisle, that sort of thing. And I'd come out, save the lady, go after Jarrett, mix it up until the WWF security guards pulled us apart. (As a last line of defense should the country ever be invaded by flesh-eating extraterrestrials, the WWF security guards rank somewhere below middle-school crossing guards.)

Fans ate it up, the ongoing battle of the sexes. There were homemade signs everywhere: CHYNA—MAKE THE SEXIST PIG SQUEAL! and MOP THE KITCHEN FLOOR WITH JARRETT'S ASS! and CHYNA SUCKS! GIVE HER A VACUUM CLEANER! Russo and his writing partner, Ed Ferrara, had a whole routine to their creative process. Russo lived in the Trumbull area, about a half-hour north of Stamford. The two writers spent mornings from nine to one watching *The Jerry Springer Show,* which was on four hours straight thanks to overlapping local TV markets. Springer's story lines were perfect for the WWF—conflict, drama, impulsive behavior, schmaltz, lots of hair-pulling, dissing—good old-fashioned dysfunction.

Over a span of about two months, the whole Jarrett-vs.-Chyna buildup became so popular that on the day that our

CHYNA

original Pay-Per-View match was supposed to take place, the WWF decided to milk the whole work for another month. They had the two of us fight, but Jarrett clobbered me with a guitar when the ref wasn't looking and "beat" me. Voilà. We have another month of getting into each other's faces.

What Vince McMahon didn't count on was Vince Russo, his top writer, "suddenly" bolting to the Ted Turner–funded WCW. So, was it Russo who "convinced" Vince McMahon to delay our match a month, knowing that Jarrett had plans to sign with the WCW—just as he did? Did Russo tip off Jarrett about Vince McMahon's intention to dump him? I'll let you be the judge.

They billed it as the Good Housekeeping match, promoted the beans out of it, and scheduled it as a Pay-Per-View feature, *No Mercy.* The date was set for October 17, 1999, in Cleveland, Ohio. Jarrett and Chyna in a title match that was really more of an extreme-type event, something New Jack would do over in the ECW league. All the holy relics of housewifery—pots, pans, vacuum cleaners, toilet seats, that kind of crap—would be laid out for us to use against each other. The kitchen sink.

Cleveland rocks, right? You have no idea . . . It was a mugging. If there had been a police report it would've read like this:

CHYNA *Nobody Holds a Grudge*

4:00 P.M. Jeff Jarrett arrives at the arena, shows ID, strolls past security. Passes a few of the guys in the halls.

"Dude, where's your gear?" Scotty Too Hotty asks him, because Jarrett doesn't have a gym bag with him.

"Don't need it." Jarrett grins, keeps walking.

4:20 P.M. Vince McMahon, managing the entire event, makes commands, gives directions, goes over the schedule. One of his assistants approaches him, I was told, as if Vince "had thorns instead of skin."

"Vince, we have a major problem with Jeff Jarrett's contract."

"He owes us another match," Vince sniffs, assuming Jarrett's fucking with him. "You tell him he wrestles or we sue the shit out of his ass."

"Uh, Vince . . . we . . . we have a *real* problem. It's not that he's refusing to perform. He's saying he *doesn't have to.* His contract's up—as of yesterday."

4:30 P.M. The fax machine in the legal department back at WWF headquarters in Stamford begins a two-hour crank job while lawyers and accountants assess the damage; in the Cleveland arena, Vince McMahon has people looking for Jeff Jarrett, who has suddenly become very elusive

CHYNA

and on the move. There are sightings up in the dining area, in the training room, and out in the parking lot. Someone said he was whistling.

4:45 P.M. I leave my hotel with visions of the championship belt, fame, money for a Dodge Viper, a Condo, TV spots, etc. At the very least, I should get a beef jerky endorsement. Okay, maybe Monistat. But things are definitely looking up.

5:10 P.M. Vince McMahon and Jeff Jarrett sit down together for the first time—alone. Whatever is said remains—for the moment—between them. Jarrett is seen walking out of the meeting with a trace of a smirk. Later, it was determined just went down. Jarrett's contract had legally lapsed, as of the day before—an oversight as big as The Big Show's hat size and, frankly, nearly as fat-headed. You can't blame Vince McMahon, either, except for trusting one employee you had done everything you could to support (Jarrett) and expecting another one, whose subsequent success could be very directly traced back to Vince himself (Russo), to be loyal. Now Jarrett was demanding to be paid to wrestle me for the Good Housekeeping match. It was a one-shot deal; the figure was rumored to be a staggering three hundred thousand dollars. Jarrett, naturally, went for the brass ring, correctly figuring there was way too much riding on the match to cancel it. Twenty thousand fans were expected to watch it live—a sellout, not to mention those across the country who had ordered the event on Pay-Per-View, and you know damn well the kind of people who order wrestling events on Pay-Per-View expect to get their money's worth. Can you spell refund?

5:30 P.M. Jarrett and Vince McMahon are in a Mexican standoff. I would've given my left breast (make that my right) to be a fly on the wall in that initial meeting when Jeff basically stuck his head in the middle of the WWF huddle and said, "Here's the deal." The thing about Vince McMahon? Family is everything, yeah. And I love that about him. But the man is competitive. Take a look at him when he walks—he leans *forward*. To find Vince McMahon you take the high road to Interstate Won, get off at Power Street, make a left on Tyranny, a right at Magnanimous, get on the low road to Persecution Complex, toss your map out the window at Self-Parody, flick on your GPS, follow the bouncing silicone, head straight out to anyplace where they take the gloves off and it's no holds barred. You don't ever beat Vince. The best you can hope for is to survive. There's

an interview I once read, that Paul Heyman gave on-line. Heyman is the head of the lesser-known ECW (Extreme Championship Wrestling) and was once a protégé of Vince McMahon's. They're still friends, and, in fact, the ECW serves as a kind of unofficial boot camp/farm club league for the WWF. The Dudley Boyz and Taz, for example, started in the ECW. So the interviewer asked Paul Heyman about Vince McMahon's notorious sense of competitiveness, if some of it might've been overblown hype.

"Listen, let me tell you something about Vince," said Heyman. "He has really thick facial hair. He can grow a full beard in a week. Shaving for him is torture. I spent time at his house, spent a weekend there once, and Vince is shaving, using an electric razor, which is twice as painful as a blade. I said something about it, like why do you put yourself through that every day, and he smiled, said something like, 'It's a reminder.' The guy is so competitive he competes with his own beard." 'Nuff said.

So Vince McMahon didn't say no to Jeff Jarrett. Didn't give in yet, but didn't say no, either. Jeff was in the building, strolling around, visiting, shooting the breeze, waiting for Vince's answer. And for Vince to not fly off the handle, to not kick Jarrett's ass all over Cleveland, then roast his furry little head on a spit, had to take every ounce of self-

CHYNA

restraint Vince McMahon could muster. It's not that he's hotheaded. He just doesn't like to lose.

5:35 P.M. I arrive at the arena and I know absolutely nothing about Jarrett's ultimatum. First thing I do is check with Pat, the booker, to see when Jarrett and I are on. Pat's a little distracted, avoids eye contact.

I am walking through the concrete bowels of the arena in all their dull grimness, but tonight, they may as well be splattered in rainbow glitter. My time, baby, my time.

Next thing I do is check in with Richie. Hunter calls him MacGyver. He's like that terrific old guy from the James Bond movies who died recently—"Q." The guy who comes up with all the nifty gadgets and toys. If I told you exactly what Richie did, I'd have to kill you, because it's a matter of trade secrets.

"So, we good with the—?" I give Richie a little hug. But suddenly everybody's acting as if I have a tree rat nesting in my hair and no one wants to tell me about it. Nobody's smiling, nobody's excited about the whole woman-getting-the-title story line. Which, come on, is a big deal. It's better than Billy Jean King whupping Bobby Riggs, because he was an old fart. It's better than Janet Guthrie being the first woman to race at the Indy 500, because they had no intention of letting her win; ditto for Geraldine Ferraro's run for the vice presidency. And I knew then how people felt about me and, damn it, I was pretty well liked. You'd think I'd get a little "You da man, Joanie!" or "Kick some ass, Joanie, you rule!" But nothing. It was like being at an embalmer's convention.

"What's going on?" I asked my friend Terry, who wrestled in Japan, where crowds never cheered and sat on their hands. She'd know what's up, how to interpret the mood.

"Maybe you should talk to Jeff." She averted her eyes.

"Talk to Jeff? What? Don't tell me he's sick . . ."

"No, he's not sick."

"Is he hurt? Fuck, he's hurt—"

I spotted Jeff, talking to Mideon near the dock exits. He looked edgy and clever, as if he had the trifecta at Saratoga locked up a day before the race. I didn't know it, but he had the whole WWF on a leash just then.

"What's going on, Jeff? Tell me something." Now, Jeff and I are good friends. He was one of the good guys, welcomed me as a performer, shared more than a few Grand Slam breakfasts with me on the road. What concerned me most right then was how fast that look of self-satisfaction and cleverness dissolved when he spotted me. I mean, it was a dead giveaway. He was up to something, he had a deal, a scheme. He felt good about the scheme except for one

CHYNA

thing—it could possibly hurt me, and he didn't feel good about that.

"Jeff—tell me what's up. I'm dying here. Everybody's acting weird. Has something changed?"

"Soon as I know something, you'll be the first one I tell. I mean that," he told me, and walked off.

6:03 P.M. Or at least that's what it was two minutes ago when I looked at my watch. Hunter comes by, touches my face. Jarrett wants money, he tells me. Somebody dropped the ball big-time and let Jarrett's contract expire—*this morning*. Which means the only thing that can make Jeff wrestle is a stack of dead presidents as high as Undertaker's bandanna. And I am crushed. I am destroyed. Use me as confetti in the next Macy's Thanksgiving Day parade, because I am in pieces.

The Pay-Per-View had been heavily promoted, so Good Housekeeping match be damned, there was gonna be wrestling. And, as the evening wore on, reality began to settle in. The truth of the matter was that *I* would be wrestling again, too, that it wasn't the end of the world as we know it. And that's what really hurt the most. I began to feel . . . normal. I began to feel *ordinary*. My great rise to the extraordinary would be fraught with the usual setbacks, struggles, dead ends, and false starts that come with the

Nobody Holds a Grudge

ordinary. All of those awful proverbs: "In the fullness of time . . ." or "Patience comes to those who wait" or, gulp, "Maybe next time . . ." I felt like a piece of shit. Then I saw him—Jarrett—coming around from behind one of the generator trailers. And he was slipping on his elbow pads.

"Let's go do this, babe. You got a little belt coming your way."

ALLLLL-FUCKING-RRRRIGHT!!!!!!!!!!

Rumor has it they paid Jarrett just a hair under a quarter of a million dollars to wrestle. I won't bore you with the details, but by all accounts it was one of the most entertaining and fun matches in WWF history. We clobbered each other with ironing boards, brooms, toasters. We called each other sexist names, scowled, worked the crowd into a Molotov cocktail, shaken and stirred, and I got the title.

So how did it feel? Everyone on their feet, color, voices, the camera in my head doing what the cameras in the arena were doing. I could see fans, mad with justice for Chyna, like they bought it, some less convinced than others but swept up in the hysteria. They made a voice, like they do for every star, and they became louder, bigger, more powerful than the star they were cheering for—the people have spoken, or some such thing. I could've been a new model of car, the unveiling of some sculpture, the forty-one-cent

CHYNA

stamp, leatherette jeans, or that woman who spent a year living up in a tree. I was a little capillary of pop culture, feeding the Always Hungry for Something New. For me? I knew all of it was an act. But I gained something I never really had before—not the belt, but respect. I made a choice, I succeeded, and I had a fucking great time doing it. And Jarrett hit me with a frozen carp.

CHINA *Nobody Holds a Grudge*

12

TV Makes You Look Smaller

You want to know who my biggest

enemy is? You want to know who gives me the most trouble, pushes my buttons, kicks my ass around the block and back? You know who gets under my skin, haunts my dreams, chews me up and spits me out more than Mommie Dearest, Colonel Von Laurer (last I heard, he had become an ex-astronaut), or any WWF wanna-be with a size 21 neck and a Captain Furious outfit? TV. TV has been berry berry good to me, I know, I know. TV gave me everything I have and I should kiss the ground it squawks on, but for the life of me, I've never been able to figure it out. It's all about family, right? TV is my beautiful older sister—prettier, smarter, more popular than me, and I hate myself for wanting to be like her. TV has a way of leading you on (Jay Leno: "Did the guys accept you?"). TV has a way of making you feel like you belong ("Pro Wrestling Puts UPN in Contention!"), until they put out the good silverware and all of a sudden every-one's looking a little closer at your invitation.

"But, darling, they're not really actors. They're, gulp . . . *wrestlers*." And, well, in some cases you can't really blame them. Despite the fact that many of us go on to become productive citizens and make positive contribu-tions to society—Jesse Ventura, governor of Minnesota! The Rock (eek!) speaking at the 2000 GOP convention— we seem to have a thing about tans, heavy metal, and

CHYNA

Norwegians. Our enhanced musculature makes it awkward for some of us to use cellular phones. Yes, the butt muscles, the butt muscles. Billy "the Caboose" Pfeiffer (not to be confused with Mr. Ass), who wrestled in the independents out of Ohio, had to be removed from a portable boat toilet by paramedics.

Most of all, we're used to expressing ourselves with great physical flourish. A scowl of hatred to someone way up in the balcony doesn't register unless your gums are showing. A smile to someone sitting thirty rows behind the

TV Makes You Look Smaller

mat is hardly noticeable unless you go ear-to-ear with it. A joker's smile. We've learned the importance of emotional projection, much the way the ancient Greeks used masks. Is it such a shock that every now and then we tend to get a little carried away? About three years ago, a couple of other women and I were doing a television interview in Toronto, *The Gallagher Show,* billed as "The Women of the WWF," or something like that. It was me; Rena Mero, the woman who plays Sable; and Debra. It started off very dignified, civil. But the interviewer had done his homework, and looking

CHYNA

back on it he baited us, really. He knew all about the bad blood between myself and Sable. And, frankly, when I think about her, I become Joanie again. I get resentful and bitter. She should've spent half of any given day thanking people and being grateful for her successes, but she didn't. Look, she had two things going for her—the WWF and the airbrush.

Armed with all that, this interviewer knew what buttons to push. He asked the obvious—why did I want to wrestle men instead of women? And I danced around it for a while, I didn't want to show up the other girls. But the guy keeps pressing me, pressing me, until Sable opens her mouth, says something like, "Chyna demeans all the women in the WWF. She thinks she's better than everyone else. I'm muscular, too, and the only reason you're bigger than the rest of us is because you choose to use illegal supplements. Riiighhht?"

"YEAH?" I'm smirking at her chest, and believe me, you can tell it's a smirk up in the thirtieth row. "LOOKS LIKE YOU'VE GOT A COUPLE SUPPLEMENTS OF YOUR OWN."

"OH, IS THAT RIGHT? YOU'VE HAD MORE PLASTIC SURGERY THAN ANYONE IN THIS ENTIRE COMPANY!" And it kind of went downhill from there. It was not a red-letter day for female wrestlers. I was

TV Makes You Look Smaller

completely embarrassed. Debra and I still laugh about it to this day. Debra made a great special referee!

So naturally, I have some reservations about accepting an invitation to the '99 Emmys. It's the T-word, and I don't mean tits. It's trust, and TV is really, really hard to trust. But screw it, what could go wrong? I am going to the Emmys. And not as Joanie. Joanie would find a way to be miserable, self-conscious, maybe even a little resentful. Didn't the judges see my guest work on *Pacific Blue*? And look at those snobby little Cousin It hairballs from *Friends*. What do they got that I ain't got? And that precious little poseur who stars in *Providence*? I could kick her ass!!! See what I mean? I was going to TV's biggest night as Chyna, and damn it, I was gonna have fun—which immediately presents a problem. Where does Chyna go to get a dress? Armani? Bill Blass? Yeah, I made six figures last year, but it was more than I had made in the previous ten years *combined*. Designer? Sure. My dress money went to Fannie Mae, the student-loan people, because I just paid off the forty grand Oscar de la Laurer saddled me with when I was back at U.T. That left shopping around, and unless you missed it, I don't exactly have the ideal body for buying off the rack. "Uh, yeah, do you have this in a size twenty on top, a five in the waist, and a six or eight in the hips?" Clothing is kind of an issue with

CHYNA

me. In the end, I went to Julie Youngberg, our WWF seamstress, to see what she could whip up in less than a month. She asked me what I had in mind, what style, what material. "You know, like, what's the theme? What look are we going for?" she asked.

"I don't know . . . something . . . wild."

"Wild is good. Leather? Maybe some sequins?"

"Well, yeah, but it can't look like I could wrestle in it or anything." My point being, I wasn't and never will be Pamela

CHYNA

Anderson, catch my drift? I wanted to go, but I didn't want to be rousted on Sunset Boulevard for solicitation.

"Okay," Julie agreed, "but are we talking cleavage? Do you want it backless?"

That's a thought. I was proud of my shoulders. You could play Chinese checkers on my rib definition.

"What about your tush? We could do a little—"

"Double hammock? Butt floss? Coupla Provolones on a rope? No, thanks."

I wanted something that said Chyna is mythical, Chyna is a bullfighter, Chyna fought in the Crusades and did battle on *Dune*. I wanted the dress to look alive, as if I had crawled into the very essence of a chimera, or a sexy gargoyle.

"Can you do that, Julie?"

"I've never seen *Dune*."

Julie worked on the dress all the way up to the Emmys. *All the way up*. In fact, she flew out to L.A. and was still gluing rhinestones on the outfit fifteen minutes before the limo was supposed to arrive. The outfit was insanely cool—this silver-and-black-leather top with a panel skirt, not a single harsh line anywhere. The whole thing worked like two halves that would join intermittently as your eyes traveled from top to bottom, a taffy pull over my body. Lots of skin—from cleavage to tummy to thigh. It looked like this incredible ink-blot test—you look at it one way and it looks like the heads of two black knights in profile; you stare at it long enough and it becomes a jackrabbit staring back at you. I looked at myself in the mirror and you know what? I wasn't Joanie, I wasn't Chyna, I was the best of both—I was . . . I was . . . Jona!!!! Listen, I'm not one of those child-bearing anarchists—Cybill, Cher, Roseanne . . . RuPaul . . . I'm not an exhibitionist. It's not my style to create a scene for the sake of spectacle. I looked at the '99 Emmys as a chance to get dressed up and mingle with my kindred spirits, even if some of them weren't cable-ready, even if I wasn't everyone's satellite dish. I still felt honored to get an invitation and considered myself show-worthy. When I got there? Walking

CHYNA

down that red carpet? All I can say is a lot of people must've seen the jackrabbit.

"I think they like your dress, Joanie," Shane McMahon said, elbowing me. Shane was my escort for the night because Hunter had to defend his championship belt at a house show. I can count the number of people who I trust on one hand. And Shane gets two fingers. He plays a heel, a coward, a dickweed in the ongoing WWF soap opera, puts himself up there for everyone to ridicule when, in reality, this guy would crawl over an acre of broken beer bottles for a friend. And talk about the T-word. Shane was the one who made good. While I was waiting for Vince McMahon to hire me, word got around. It's really no different from industrial espionage. The two behemoths are the WWF and Ted Turner's WCW, and they're like the Hatfields and the McCoys, Ford vs. General Motors, Spy vs. Spy. They steal, copy, insult, rip on, sabotage each other at every turn. If you put Vince McMahon in a room with Eric Bishoff (Bishoff runs the company for Turner), they'd play kickball with each

TV Makes You Look Smaller

other's heads. So I'd be asking, "When? When? When is Vince McMahon gonna give me a shot?" "Joanie, just hang on," Shane would tell me. "I'm working on it, I'm working on it." But the WCW had just created NWO—the New World Order, a bunch of ultra-bad guys, this hard-guy Mafia of rule-breakers. I got a call from one of their bookers. They wanted me to be the only chick in the New World Order; they were excited about having this ass-kicking rebel bitch hanging with the dudes. A modern Fat Albert crew with a major attitude. Hey, hey, hey, mother-fuckaaaa! The WCW had this event in Alabama and they wanted me to come down, meet with them. And the timing for me was pretty sweet, because I had planned to fly down to the Florida Keys to visit my gonzo friend, Bev, and to see Hunter, who was wrestling in a WWF Pay-Per-View, as it happened (ha!) up in Palm Beach. When I got down to the Keys, Bev offered to keep me company for the fifteen-hour drive to Alabama; along the way we could stop, say hi to Hunter in West Palm Beach.

Now, Pay-Per-View events are intense. It's live television, so everybody's in siege mode with a little preamp of panic. Nobody's interested in making small talk or chasing big ideas around in the air. "Not now" is the mantra, because this big, ten-million-dollar high school play called *King of the Ring* or *Summer of Slam* is about to go live.

CHYNA

Backstage for the Palm Beach PPV, while I'm wishing Hunter good luck, out of the corner of my eye I spot Shane coming at me. Part of Shane's charm comes from his perpetual anxiousness; hang around him and you get the feeling that you're on a thrill ride clicking up to the top. Little things excite and delight him; with Shane, you're on a perpetual road trip. And he loves fashion. A plus in my book! He touches my arm, pulls me aside.

"I heard you're going to Alabama." He spoke in a low, conspiratorial voice. Hunter, the sly devil, must've *let it slip*. "I'm telling you right now. Don't go there."

"Oh? Are you guaranteeing me a job?"

"I'm telling you not to go to Alabama because it'll be too late and you'll totally regret it."

"Then you *are* offering me a job!"

"Joaniieeee." Shane's moaning, wringing his hands, acting as if I asked him to sneak me into his father's dressing room.

"But you just winked—"

"No, I didn't. I didn't wink. Okay, I winked. But it was a moral-support wink, not a you're-hired wink."

"They're gonna hire me now, Shane."

"So are we. Just, please, hang on. Vince is this close"— he made a tweezers with his fingers—"and if you go up there and work for them you won't be a fresh face for the

CHYNA

WWF, and the one thing Vince prides himself on is *making* stars. He doesn't steal . . . very often. He makes stars. I promise you. If you hang on, we'll make you a star here."

Now, I've come to understand that before these PPV performances, most of the folks involved become pod people. And for Shane to take time out and make that kind of passionate appeal to me, well, I was sold. I didn't go up to Alabama and Shane made good on his promise. And I'll never forget him for it.

All right then. Emmy, Emmy, who's got the Emmy? Shane has his arm entwined with mine — the perfect gentleman, dressed to the nines, and we are in the mingle stream, chins up. If ever there was a night I felt like Cinderella, that was it! Let me tell you something about ground zero. As in calories. Most of the women here look like they eat every other day. Saltines. Celery casserole. As in if you tip the scales anywhere north of one hundred pounds, you're Rosie O'Donnell. I'm afraid to shake hands with some of them for fear of tearing off an arm. I have my camera. If I can muster the nerve, I'm thinking about grabbing Calista Flockhart and Camryn Manheim, having Shane snap my picture with them. I could offer it up as the new cover to *Our Bodies, Ourselves, Volume 20.*

And the teeth. Chicklet-white. *Straight.* You could use Jenna Elfman's smile to draw blueprints. Shane and I are

TV Makes You Look Smaller

making our way past all the interviewers; the ushers (obviously tipped off) herd us away from the network types and into that one-two gauntlet, Joan Rivers and her daughter, Melissa, covering the Emmys for the E! Channel.

"Here's the terribly funny Sarah Jessica Parker," Melissa Rivers coos. We're just behind them. Here is the terribly underfed Sarah Jessica Parker, so tiny, so hospital-bed thin that if somebody sneezes she could blow away. While Melissa fawns over Sarah Jessica, her husband, Matthew Broderick, graciously backs away. Maybe the sheer grandness of it all made him forget that there might be other people there, I don't know, but Matthew, who stands maybe five-seven without the Inspector Gadget hat, backs himself into the flesh-exposed land between the two halves of my dress—which is to say, he parked between my boobs. At first, I felt a little bad for him because he just seemed to get so flustered. He bobbed at the very last second, kind of like a fighter ducking a punch, but the tip of his nose caught the right-side seam of my dress. My lord, the hot breath of a movie star, dissolving the glue of my rhinestones! To his credit, he tried to act like it never happened, but in trying to pivot away from my juggage, he stepped on my foot. Didn't hurt. I mean the guy weighs, what, thirty-four pounds wet? He gives me that wonderful Ferris Bueller "can't be helped" shrug.

Truth be told, I think the whole scene made him a little uncomfortable. But behind the cutesy Ferris Bueller expression I could see astonishment and alarm crashing around in his eyes, like there but by the grace of God, or that look people get when they see farm animals fucking off the side of the highway and they hope the kids don't ask about it. Like, oh, my God, they've landed and they're among us! There goes the food supply. It's . . . it's . . . one of those . . . wrestlers. Anyway, forgive me, but I decided to have a little fun.

"You stepped on my foot," I said, unsmiling.

"Excuse me?"

"I said, you stepped on my foot. Don't do it again."

Matthew kneads the air in front of him with his palms—easy, big fella. "Oh, gee," he apologizes, "I'm, I'm really, really sorry—"

"You should be." I cut him off, and he disappeared between a crack in the crowd. Shane and I giggled. I saw his hand pop back through as an afterthought, latching on to Sarah Jessica Parker's wrist and pulling her through the crack with him. Later on, I'm in the ladies' room and I'm washing my hands. I think it was after I shook hands with somebody that by looking at them you're certain they jerk off more than normal. There is Sarah Jessica Parker, using the sink next to me.

CHINA *TV Makes You Look Smaller*

"You know, you really scared the living daylights out of my husband," she laughingly tells me.

"I did?"

"Yeah. Totally."

"Oh, I'm sorry. You make sure to tell him I was just joking."

"I'll try. Just . . . please don't do that to him again?" She said in the form of a question, so serious, so . . . HBO-like. Well, forget it, baby, 'cause you're on cable just like me.

By now, you know I'm pretty tough, pretty resilient, right? Especially as Chyna. You gotta get some shoulder behind that needle and push it through some serious skin before you hit a vein, before you can get to me—or at least before I'll show it. And there was plenty to bawl about. The slights, getting passed on for a *SmackDown!*, or working and having people spitting on you, the exotic beer shampoos, people asking to see your dick, little kids calling you a cunt, the aches, the pains, the foam-rubber motel pillows, the big, dark shadow of my estranged family (of course!), the loneliness. Especially in the beginning, when I first joined the WWF—lotta swallowed tears. I wanted to be perceived as someone who could handle all of it, not this high-maintenance, hormonal, sniffly *problem*. I guess if I had any real designs on competing with the guys, I had to act like one. Damnedest thing, isn't it?

CHYNA

So Shane and I sidle up to Melissa Rivers. And what happened next was a real test for me. I could see right off that Melissa had no idea who I was and already had that puppet nose of hers in the air over my dress. We made eye contact and it wasn't a good vibe at all. She's thinking, "In your dreams, Godzilla," and I'm thinking, "Oh, yeah, got the runoff from Mama's fame, right? You're just dying to trot off somewhere and snicker about me, but you gotta stand there with that microphone, so suck it up, girl, and get on with the healing." They had one camera for both Joan and Melissa Rivers and they did this tag-team thing. One would prepare an interview while the other did one with the camera. While the camera's on Joan, a publicist introduces me: Melissa, this is Chyna, blah, blah, blah. The camera turns to us, the light goes red, Melissa looks into it and announces, "We're going to take a short break now, be right back." She makes the cutoff sign to the cameraman, then turns her back on me, the little bitch.

I admit it, I was crushed. I had a lump in my throat the size of a cantaloupe and the dress, the energy, the excitement of being there hemorrhaged out of me. Joanie came out of suspension from Chyna; you could see the sediment in the glass. It was humiliating, and Shane, my soul brother, steered me away, put his arms around me. "It's okay, Joanie, don't worry. You rocked the place tonight."

CHYNA

Two things of consequence happened a few days later. One, I wound up on Mr. Blackwell's worst-dressed list for the Emmys. And that was heartening. Blackwell has the worst taste on earth, which meant my dress was really cool. Or was it? Maybe it sucked. Maybe I was bad taste wrapped in cellophane, I don't know . . .

The best part, though, was going back to work. Shane told everybody what went down with Melissa Rivers.

"What? You're shitting me." Perry Saturn turned bright red under his tan. "That piece of cardboard did that to you?"

Big Show: "Fuck. If I'm ever at the Emmys and she interviews me, I'll shove that mike up her ass and into her brainpan!"

Kane: "Good luck finding it. Hey, Joanie, say the word and we'll find the bitch and shit in her bag."

God, I love those guys.

Dear friends, I'm kind of on a roll here, so if I can indulge you all a little longer, I'm going to stay with this TV-as-my-noble-adversary thing for the moment. And I stand corrected. Television isn't my prettier older sister. It's my prettier girlfriend, the one I envy, the one I have to compete with, the one who always gets the date. Let me give you an example and then, I promise, I'll go hide my tears in the shower.

CHYNA

TV Makes You Look Smaller

December 1998 "So . . . (huff, puff) what do you want for Christmas?" Hunter asks me. He's all sweaty, really working it.

"Well (oh, oh), can I combine my birthday with Christmas?" I can feel my legs starting to tingle, like they're going rubbery.

"I was gonna do that anyway," he tells me, his face straining. "Hey, hey, slow down a little, okay? Do you always have to outlift me?"

We're pumping iron, bench press. *I was gonna do that anyway* . . . figures. I've been getting gypped for years having my birthday combined with Christmas. Okay. Be that way. Then I'm going for broke.

"Take me to Vegas," I said.

"Vegas."

"Yeah. You know how much I love the shows. Let's just go somewhere together, alone, where we can watch other people for once. Please? Vegas? Christmas, birthday, and you can throw in Valentine's Day," I offered. He gave me the Hunter squint, which meant "Sure, kid, you know I love ya." Then he told me he was gonna throw in Valentine's anyway.

We have the tickets! A suite at the MGM Grand! (Not my first choice, but who's complaining?) I have my little blackjack card, telling me when to double-down, split, take

CHYNA

insurance. Two days before our flight, Hunter walks in the room.

"Joanie, guess what!?" He's clutching my arms, excited in a self-conscious way that makes me suspect that he secretly thinks he should be more excited than he is, you follow me? He's guilty about something and I have a decision to make. Should I play along, even though I know it has something to do with the vacation—i.e., we're not going to Vegas? Should I play along just to give him a little practice? I do this, you know, when he's about to give me a load of bullshit—just let him ramble on because it's beneficial to his acting career. And I have to say his work has really improved. Case in point: He really looks married to Stephanie McMahon, doesn't he? But this time I was just too tired to play along, so I ended it right there.

"We're not going to Vegas, right?"

"Well—we're gonna go, we're gonna go, sure, sure," he sputtered. "It's just been postponed a little. I'll take you another time, that's all. First we're gonna go to L.A.! I got asked to appear on *The Drew Carey Show*. Isn't that great?"

It *was* great, even if it meant putting a hold on our vacation plans. *Drew Carey* was one of the top sitcoms and it would be great exposure for Hunter; I knew that and I was genuinely happy for him. At one time, where Hunter went,

TV Makes You Look Smaller

I went, and vice versa, so on to L.A., the only city on earth that seems built on a soap bubble.

We go to the set for the shoot. Hunter has a few days of rehearsal; it's like the entire cast and crew is in awe of him. And what not to be in awe of? They should love him because he is truly one of the most attractive people I know (and when I say attractive, I don't mean just looks; Hunter's got charisma by the ton).

How should I say this, especially with my imagination, my emotional baggage, my issues? It seemed like I was getting the cold shoulder on the set. Lots of stiff smiles; production people whose body language gave off a vibe of exaggerated patience. You know the attitude — it's that free-bie thing that the word "complimentary" was invented for. I was along for the ride. Fine, I could deal with that. It was Hunter's scene. And, like I say, I could've been imagining it.

The show was taped before a live audience. Hunter's bit involved a wrestling-style interview that worked his character. We arrived a few hours before the show, just to get a feel for the place, you know, get acquainted.

"You look a little tight, hon." I put my arms around Hunter. "You okay? You want me to make you a protein shake?"

They had me do a little walk-on cameo (how nice — no, really), taped before Hunter's performance and the actual

CHYNA

live show—they'd edit in my walk-on in postproduction. It was a big night for the show. All the extras were there, family, friends. On our side, our manager, Barry, was there, along with some friends, a high-level executive from the Disney studio, other fairly big players, all there to see Hunter. Just before the live taping began, some production manager approaches me, and my manager, Barry, informs us that we'll be watching the show from a monitor in this dinky little trailer. Now the audience, the extras, the execs, the friends, friends of friends, they're all out on the set. Yeah, I felt a little dissed, but Joanie, the good soldier, retreated back to that trailer, settled in with the microwave popcorn, the miniature Scotchgarded couch, and the ever-present bathroom-door mirror put up specially so stars can watch themselves crap. They did have a pot of curry chicken there for us! Just my luck because even the smell of curry makes me want to vomit. I stuck with the popcorn for dinner that night. Let's see, how's that go? I'm a uniter, not a divider. So Barry and I took turns exhaling curry chicken fumes (that's how small the trailer was) and watched the show. And Hunter just burned the house down, I mean he was really good. Applause, applause, lights up, Barry and I squeeze ourselves out of the trailer, trot up to the set to join Hunter.

"So?" he asks.

"Oh, babe, you did so great."

TV Makes You Look Smaller

"It was good?" He knew it was good, but I would've done the same thing tenfold.

"Really good. Barry's running down copies of it. Hunter, you rocked. We're so proud of you!" Now there's a pocket of people forming around Hunter, everybody talking at once, and I feel this limp hand on my wrist.

"Chyna, can I speak with you for a sec?" This guy who identified himself as one of the assistant directors of the show (by my count, there were now thirty-five) finds a point that seems to focus across the room and on the bridge of Drew Carey's horn-rimmed glasses — really, I had to look, because he refused to make eye contact. He's talking to Drew Carey's glasses, and really fast, too.

"You'll-have-to-leave-the-set-I've-been-instructed-to-escort-you-off-I'm-sorry-can-you-follow?"

"Excuse me?" My back went up — just a little. "Because for a second there I thought you said 'You'll have to leave the set, I've been instructed to escort you off, I'm sorry, can you follow' — "

"They're asking you to leave the set," the assistant director pro tem quickly adjusted, did this nice little sit-out, using "they" as his escape move. Hunter, dreaming of his own series as a wrestling private eye, drifts back to reality long enough to hear the assistant director repeat himself.

CHYNA

"What's he saying, what's he saying?" He's gesturing to his ear, as if he can't hear.

"He's saying they want me to leave the set, Hunter."

Hunter's chest goes into gorilla position. "For what?" He's glaring—YEAH—until that pocket of people swallows him up in compliments now—"Beautiful, Hunter, great show! Great show!"—and I find myself following this assistant-to-the-hand-holder-of-the-director, allowing this ass-face with nothing to his name but a VIP pass to the CityWalk Hard Rock, this . . . this Wet Vac to suck the will to live out of me. Jesus, it's like being led out of the building by a preschooler. Everyone's watching, too—hey, I'm Chyna, not Dr. Fucking Ruth! I'm *visible,* know what I'm saying here? So, I go in shame—and boy, does shame like me. If shame is a piece of used gum, I am the underside of a chair. "Joanie, you gotta stand up straight," the great psychoanalyst Sigmund Laurer used to scold me when I was living with him (likely off of someone else's hard-earned pay). "You have to be proud of your body. Tall chicks are cool." Yeah? Well, right now I wish I was frigging Thumbelina, all right—*DADDY?* "From the time she was two she always had a bright, lovely smile on her face." Yeah, well, I ain't a-smiling now. Here I am, following this guy, going quietly, slinking off without a peep. The assistant-to-the-second-alternate-pro-tem-director escorted me to Hunter's trailer

TV Makes You Look Smaller

and, bless his chilly little heart, he felt for me—but not enough to put himself in jeopardy by saying something that could possibly enter into the TV-biz ether, where it could take shape and bite him in his flat ass. That's the other thing about TV—the people behind it are driven by Dread. Like I said, *family*.

"Sucks," the little fella with the tasseled loafers and the earpiece askew muttered with a shrug—which could mean anything from me getting the heave-ho to Drew Carey's choice of eyewear. So what? Don't kill the messenger. I know. I'll kill Hunter.

Five minutes alone and I am on a crying jag that could rival an Italian funeral, my face wild-horse contorted, mascara turned loose all over my face in a black torrent. Yeah, the humiliation opened the floodgates, but anger made the tears hot. I was such a pansy for going along with the whole thing. They booted me off the set and I should've stood up to them—fuck you, you're not kicking me out of here! But I didn't. I let them diss me. The voice. Momma's voice: Don't make waves, Joanie. You could queer your future, Joanie. It's Hunter's night, don't rain on his parade, Joanie. So I did what Joanie does best—complete and utter capitulation. Lower, Joanie, your belly's not touching the ground.

"Dear Hunter," I scrawled on some network stationery, "I'm going home." Signed it. *Home*. Nice touch, huh? I

CHYNA

meant back to the hotel, but I can be an effective bitch, just like the conceited female star (I won't name names) who allegedly was behind the directive to have me booted. Seems she felt I was stealing some of her much-undeserved attention. "Oh, oh, oh, what if E.T. decides to talk to the Amazon Woman instead of little young me?" Whatever. *Home*. That'll keep him guessing, the worm. The 255-pound, buffed worm. I looked in the mirror: leopard coat, tight spandex pants, high heels, groovy ponytail. I looked hot. What a waste.

I get in my car, drive for about a half a mile, then STAND ON THE FUCKING BRAKES, a rooster plume of acrid tire smoke skirting the car (it's a rental). Unh-uh. No way. I'm not leaving like this. I'm going back to that cliqueish fucking set, and if they want me to leave, they can pick me up and carry me. Chyna's back, and Chyna parked right in some big shot's spot. (Of course, like almost everybody else, he was probably gone for the day, but if he *did* come back, watch out!) I'm out of the car like a shot, stalking for the set, when somebody whistles. Probably a security guard. Just try and stop me, screw!

"JOANIE! HEY, JOANIE!" It's Hunter, with Barry and Mitch, the Disney executive. All I saw was Hunter; all I saw was bright red.

TV Makes You Look Smaller

"Joanie—we've been looking all over for you. Where'd you run off to?"

"You're kidding, aren't you?"

"Well, they said you were in the trailer—"

"THEY SAID I HAD TO LEAVE, TOO. Did you hear that part, Hunter? They can't treat me like this! I'm going back in there!"

"Baby, calm down—"

"Calm down??? They humiliated me! They made a sap out of me in front of a large group of people, Hunter! All those puny, half-starved, cigarette-smoking assholes! What are they doing there, besides fighting over whose cock they can suck for a raise? AND I'M NOT YOUR FUCKING GROUPIE, HUNTER!"

Wow, that felt good. And the best part was that after acting like I needed an exorcist and making a complete ass out of myself, Hunter didn't break up with me. Because *I* would've broken up with me.

A couple days later I'm back on the road with the gang—I think we were in Minneapolis. Everyone's coming up to me, incredulous.

"Wait a minute, wait a minute"—Big Show rolls his eyes—"you got kicked off the *Drew Carey* set? For what?"

"Jealousy."

CHYNA

"Oh, my God, Drew Carey's jealous of you?" X-Pac tensed up. He has to be one of the most loyal, kindhearted guys on the tour—he feels for you, and I always like that. But on the gullibility scale, he's off the board.

"No, no . . . some tight-ass with an expense account and a knack for sword swallowing thought I was stealing her thunder."

"Wow, Chyna"—Big Show's scratching at whiskers that don't exist—"some women, like, have a real problem with you, don't they? Like, what is it? What's wrong with them?"

Simple, my wonderful, ravioli-hawking friend. They want me to have a dick, and preferably not one of theirs.

TV Makes You Look Smaller

13

Maybe They Did Know

I love zeros! I mean, the year 2000

put one hell of a bulge in my little sack of life. There were highs and lows, the moments were sweet and sour, but never dull, which is always good for my complexion (when I get bored, I eat too much chocolate). On the personal side, I broke up with Hunter. We're still very close, but I bought some land on which I intend to build a home and have a swimming pool shaped like his ass. Speaking of asses, I went on the *Howard Stern Show* and probably made one out of myself. Look at the freak, look at the freak, right? Big shoulders, big legs, big arms, big hands—with a big middle finger on each one. Anyway, I sat there, let them trot me around like a circus pony, answered the snickering questions while Robin and Stuttering John and Jackie and Fred giggled like a bunch of campfire girls who wandered onto the Chicks with Dicks website. It's supposed to be about no boundaries, no inhibitions, when really, the whole show is all about concealment. It was like, well . . . it was like being home: the manufactured controversy, the phony ill-will, the organ humor, tits on the forebrain, the stale bagels. It was the WWF with headphones and more commercials—the gloves are off, nobody gets hurt, and everybody wins.

"Oh, yeah, I think I dig you, the more I look at you," Howard went all basso profundo into the mike. "Yeah,

CHYNA

yeah, I'd do you, definitely." Maybe I could get it up for him, I don't know . . . As much as I liked him, in a best-case scenario, I have a feeling he'd be jacking my hair extensions all the time. "Yeah, I can see us together," he went on, the point here having nothing to do with my sexuality, attractiveness, and disposition—or his, for that matter. It was Howard's way of hiding his self-consciousness (here is a man who should sprinkle Paxil on his shredded wheat every morning) because in the end he wanted to be liked and that, dear friends, is a wish that transcends chromosomes.

I had to read in *Talk* magazine how my mother thinks I'm taking mushrooms; in the same article that ex-boyfriend of mine (Jerry) says, "People used to make fun of her big jaw and her nose and accuse her of being on steroids, which wasn't true, but I loved everything about her." And he wonders why he's an ex. At least I got to keep the clothes from the photo shoot. I still haven't spoken to my mother, which is sad, but nothing's ever exactly the way we want it to be. As for my dad, if there's an island just waiting to be turned into a launch pad for private satellites, he'll be there. If there's a professional women's topless curling league to be started, he'll be there. If there's a group of foreign diplomats to be had, or a tribe of East Africans dying to get into the record business, he'll be there. My sister, Kathy, had a baby; my brother, Sonny, came to see me wrestle. On the professional

CHYNA *Maybe They Did Know*

side, I lost the intercontinental belt, became Eddie Guerrero's ultimate woman, then won the belt back, which was
nice and would've been even nicer had I not been locked out
of my hotel room that night. I had to sleep in the car—some
things never change. And Chyna gets an endorsement! I did
a few Stacker 2 fat-burner commercials, then attended the

CHYNA

Democratic convention and covered my eyes like everyone else when Al Gore played tonsil hockey with Tipper in front of a hundred million people. In September, I was a guest presenter for the MTV Music Awards. And speaking of mushrooms, they paired me up with popular culture's latest toadstool, *Survivor*'s Richard Hatch. The writers gave us this awful bit. We threw away the script and vamped, which was cool—until I split my pants.

Oh. And did I tell you I'm pregnant? Okay, I'm not, but I did pose nude for *Playboy,* and talk about "if they only knew." First of all, let me say that it's the weirdest feeling on Hef's

heaving earth to be stark naked, spread-eagled in front of someone while they're trying to "light" your crotch ever so perfectly. Glamour? Milking a cow with your feet is more glamorous than leaning forward on all fours while a guy standing behind you shines a spotlight on your ass. I saw the Polaroids first. We needed to pick and choose, and frankly, an in-depth analysis of my genitalia is not what I consider a day well spent. Some were nice. Others had a bit too

CHYNA

much of the Black Forest region and Bigfoot showing for my taste, but, hey, it's all business, right? The business of beaver, and being the professional that I am, I held my end up (no pun intended). Next came the all-important shower scene. This is where I had to carefully wash one tit in ecstasy with my eyes closed. All told, I was given a whopping twelve pages, which must've had the airbrush guy seeing dollar signs. They told me afterward that very little retouching would be required; if they were just trying to flatter me, tough titty—I took it as the truth and decided to reward myself. Since throughout my successes I've never received any flowers, jewels, or even spectacular romantic dates, I splurged and bought a fur coat—at a summer sale price, of course! And before anyone accuses me of cruelty to animals, just remember I haven't said one unkind word about Sable.

Not long ago somebody asked me how it felt to be at the whim of someone else, to have someone control my fate. Someone who, at any time, could decide that Joanie needs to be hospitalized, chastised, or sent away; wear a clown suit, go blind, rise from the ashes, fight a Brahma bull, retire, come back. Well, without question, it's hard, most of all because I love what I do. You hear the nagging unhappiness in the way someone will drag a can across the sidewalk or rattle their fingers over a computer keyboard. You see it on freeways, all the hot, tired, unfulfilled faces fighting off

the glare of having to do something they despise. You feel it when you walk into a room of suits, how much they'd rather be alone instead of entertaining a roomful of bad notions and worse ideas. Look, we all want to be the proprietors of our own fate, we all want to *own,* but when all is said and done, most of us end up renting. That would be me—renter. Tenant to the home of my own future. Unfurnished. If it ended tomorrow, hey, there's always . . . politics.

Still, I'll say it again. I love what I do. I come to work, I can smell popcorn and sports cream, the air peculiar to whatever city we happen to be in—the moss in Cleveland, the clay in Santa Fe, the yeast in Milwaukee. I get to toss around a lot of great-looking guys, have Jan the makeup lady do my hair, and wince without hurting. I have places to go that give me comfort, friends who give me strength, and a family that gives me fits, to be sure. But for me, there's one place I'm no longer afraid of—being in front of a mirror. For most of my life I have been showing one face to the world and living with another, conflicted and hidden. And that's not entirely fixed yet. But for once I can look at myself and see someone smiling back. And I *am* smiling.

CHYNA

Acknowledgments

To my sister, Kathy—remember, Kath, I'm a lifetime commitment.

A special thank you to the McMahons and to all the people who have worked behind the scenes at the WWF to help make me a success. I appreciate you all.

To "the boys" (and "the girls" too): The best years of my life and all of my greatest achievements have been shared with you. You are all truly the most driven, kindest, frustrating, attractive, and talented group of people I have ever known. Thank you. I love you guys.

To my little buddy Blitz: Aunt Joanie loves you.

Thanks to Judith Regan and all of the staff at ReganBooks. This book is so special to me. It has been a lifelong dream to tell my story. Thank you.

Captions

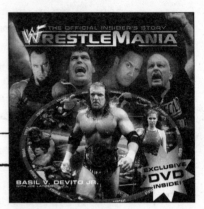